Engels 200

– his contribution to political economy

Engels 200

– his contribution to political economy

Michael Roberts

Engels 200
– his contribution to political economy
© Michael Roberts 2020

Cover design and layout: Eva Kinch Hall, Ordered by Colour
Published and printed by Lulu.com
Printed in London, UK 2020

ISBN: 978-1-716-47133-9

Contents

Engels 200

This short book has been written to coincide with the 200th anniversary of the birth of Friedrich Engels, the close friend and collaborator with Karl Marx for over 40 years. This book is not a biography of Engels – there are plenty of those, of varying quality. Instead, it aims to outline, explain and analyse Engels' contribution to a Marxist critique of political economy and capitalism. Engels' economics has been sadly neglected, being lost under the large shadow of Marx's Capital and his other economic works. And yet, Engels was the first to present a critique of the contemporary classical political economy of Smith, Ricardo and Malthus from a Marxist perspective – that is before Marx himself.

Engels first coined several concepts and categories of Marxist economic theory that are usually associated with Marx. But after realising that Marx had much more to contribute to an analysis of capitalism than he, Engels took a back seat. He did this for two main reasons. First, he was working for his father's cotton manufacturing firm in Manchester for over 20 years (from about 1850), so he had little time to write anything substantial of his own, apart from helping Marx in writing articles under Marx's name; providing criticism and information; and collaborating on political activity.

Second, because he was working and was indeed a junior partner in the firm, Engels received a sufficient income to live well, while also subsidising Marx and his family so that Marx could work (very slowly!) on his economics, leading eventually to the publication of Capital, his major work.

In a way, Engels lived a double life: a respectable bourgeois factory boss (not really, more a glorified clerk) associating with the Manchester cotton barons' families in sport and social activity; and at the same time living with a working-class activist in various less salubrious residences, researching and writing his own works on a scientific explanation of the need to overthrow capitalism.

When Engels retired from his job in 1870, he moved down London to a house very close to the Marx family home to allow regular contact with his lifetime friend. And he resumed his own economic and political writings, making several important publications over the next decade or so before Marx's death in 1883.

After Marx's death, Engels set himself the task of publishing the rest of Marx's work on Capital. Marx had originally envisaged that Capital would have up to ten volumes covering all aspects of capitalism. That was eventually shrunk down to three or four. But Marx had never proceeded to complete these further volumes, spending his time on editing Volume One in new editions, writing many other works and articles and participating in political activity. So it fell on Engels to turn a mountain of notes left by Marx into what were eventually Volumes 2 and 3 of Capital. They were published just before Engels' death in 1895.

In those years after Marx's death, Engels also added his own important contributions to Marxist political economy, including sensitive insights into the trends in late 19th century capitalism and prescient forecasts of its future. And he became, as he said himself, the main defender of Marxism within the mass labour movements developing at the time against all the other competing theories of socialism. In doing so, he provided a much more systematic popular explanation of Marxism or 'scientific socialism'. Indeed, it could be said that because Engels was so convincing in his analyses that many people since have sought to claim that Engels distorted Marx's ideas into his own simplistic, 'determinist' views.

This book will outline Engels' important contributions to political economy and will show that it would be difficult to put a sheet of paper between his economics and that of Marx. Moreover, even now, Engels' critique of capitalism is still relevant and compelling. Indeed, this book should be seen as a companion to Marx 200, a book I wrote to coincide with Marx's own 200th birthday anniversary in 2018. There are references to that book throughout this one. References to Engels' works will be found in the bibliography. And the sources for all charts will also be found at the end of this book.

In the first chapter, I outline a brief biography of Engels, measuring his value to Marxian political economy. In chapter two, I look at Engels' ground-breaking early critique of classical political economy, well before

Marx. In chapter three, I consider the content of Engels' major work of economic and social analysis of rising British capitalist production in the so-called industrial revolution and its impact on labour – in so doing proposing for the first time some laws of accumulation under capitalism that Marx took up and developed. In chapter four, I show how Engels was the first to consider the law of value as proposed by the classical bourgeois economists and to provide a Marxist critique. Chapter five will explain how after Marx's death, Engels defended it against allcomers and expounded what Marx called 'the most important law in political economy', the law of the tendency of the rate of profit to fall. Chapter six looks at Engels' contributions to the economic analysis of capitalism after Marx's death, in particular on cycles of booms and slumps, impe-rialism and military spending and the transition to socialism. Chapter seven sums up his overall contribution to Marxian political economy 200 years since his birth.

The price of Engels

Half the price

In May 2018, at the time of the 200th anniversary of the birth of Karl Marx, an auction took place in Beijing. Up for sale was just one page of notes that Marx made for his seminal work, Capital. It included extracts and analyses that Marx made on British banker James William Gilbart's book "Practical Treatise on Banking," which he referenced when writing his piece "Capital: Critique of Political Economy."

Chinese billionaire, Feng Lun jumped in to buy this original page of Marx's illegible script in German for 3.34m yuan or $523,000. Such was the 'value' of Marx's name and work in the eyes of a Chinese billionaire.

At the same auction, a manuscript by Marx's long-standing friend and collaborator, Friedrich Engels also came up for sale. It was an article that

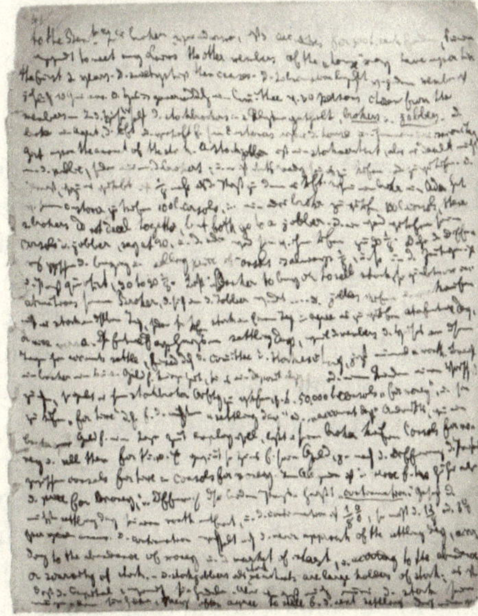

Marx's undecipherable script

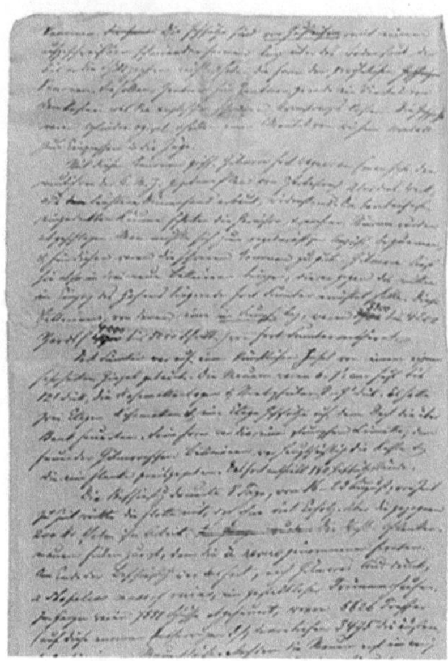

Engels' elegant writing

Engels wrote for the newspaper, Allgemeine Militärzeitung in November 1862. It was sold for exactly half the price of Marx's script, 1.67 million yuan.

So Engels' contribution to what he and Marx called 'scientific socialism' was exactly half that of Marx's – at least according to prices in that auction. Was that a fair measure? Well, as Oscar Wilde once said: "If a cynic knows the price of everything but the value of nothing, then a romantic must be a man who knows the value of everything but the price of nothing." When it comes to Engels, I am a romantic. This short book will attempt to promote the contribution that Engels made to Marxist political economy and scientific socialism. Engels' work in collaborating with Marx in philosophy, anthropology, journalism and revolutionary politics has been well documented by a host of authors. But the value of his work in political economy has been relatively neglected. And yet, in many ways Engels was ahead of Marx in developing Marxist economic theory, in observing and analysing important trends in capitalist economies and in developing revolutionary economic policies. In my view, being priced at half Marx's contribution is much too low an estimate.

The young Engels

Engels was born on 28 November 1820 at Barmen-Elberfeld, a Prussian province of the Rhineland, which in 1930 was renamed Wuppertal as a city in North Rhine-Westphalia. He was the eldest son of Friedrich Engels Sr. (1796–1860) and of Elisabeth "Elise" Franziska Mauritia von Haar (1797–1873). The wealthy Engels family owned large cotton-textile mills in Barmen and Salford, both expanding industrial metropoles. Friedrich's parents were devout Pietist Protestants and they raised their children accordingly.

At the age of 13, Engels attended grammar school in the adjacent city of Elberfeld but had to leave at 17, due to pressure from his father, who wanted him to become a businessman and start to work as a mercantile apprentice in his firm. After a year in Barmen, the young Engels was in 1838 sent by his father to undertake an apprenticeship at a commercial house in Bremen. His parents expected that he would follow his father into a career in the family business.

The Engels family house at Barmen (now in Wuppertal), Germany

Engels at 19 years old

Whilst at Bremen, Engels began reading the philosophy of Hegel, whose teachings dominated German philosophy at that time. In September 1838, Engels published his first work, a poem entitled "The Bedouin", in the Bremisches Conversationsblatt. He also engaged in other literary work and began writing newspaper articles critiquing the societal ills of industrialisation. He wrote under the pseudonym "Friedrich Oswald" to avoid connecting his family with his provocative writings.

In 1841, Engels performed his military service in the Prussian Army as a member of the Household Artillery. Assigned to Berlin, he attended university lectures at the University of Berlin and began to associate with groups of Young Hegelians. He anonymously published articles in the Rheinische Zeitung, exposing the poor employment and living-conditions endured by factory workers. The editor of the Rheinische Zeitung was Karl Marx, but Engels would not meet Marx until late November 1842. Engels acknowledged the influence of German philosophy on his intellectual development throughout his career. He also wrote, "To get the most out of life you must be active, you must live and you must have the courage to taste the thrill of being young ... " (1840).

Engels the revolutionary

Engels developed atheistic beliefs and his relationship with his parents became strained. In 1842, his parents sent the 22-year-old Engels to Manchester, England, a manufacturing centre where industrialisation was on the rise. He was to work in Weaste in the offices of Ermen and Engels' Victoria Mill, which made sewing threads. Engels's father thought that working at the Manchester firm might make his son reconsider some of his radical opinions. On his way to Manchester, Engels visited the office of the Rheinische Zeitung in Cologne and met Karl Marx for the first time. They were not impressed with each other. Marx mistakenly thought that Engels was still associated with the Berliner Young Hegelians, with whom Marx had just broken off ties.

In Manchester, Engels met Mary Burns, a fierce young Irish woman with radical opinions who worked in the Engels factory. They began a relationship that lasted 20 years until her death in 1863. The two never married, as both were against the institution of marriage. While Engels regarded stable monogamy as a virtue, he considered the current state and church-regulated marriage as a form of class oppression.

Burns guided Engels through Manchester and Salford, showing him the worst districts for his research. While in Manchester between October and November 1843, Engels wrote his first economic work, entitled Outline of a Critique of Political Economy (Umrisse). Engels sent the work to Paris, where Marx published it in the Deutsch–Französische Jahrbücher in 1844.

While observing the slums of Manchester in close detail, Engels took notes of its horrors, notably child labour, the despoiled environment, and overworked and impoverished labourers. He sent a trilogy of articles to Marx. These were published in the Rheinische Zeitung and then in the Deutsch–Französische Jahrbücher, chronicling the conditions among the working class in Manchester.

He later collected these articles for his influential first book, The Condition of the Working Class in England (1845)- to be called The Condition for short in this book. In the book, Engels described the "grim future of capitalism and the industrial age", noting the details of the squalor in which the working people lived. The book was not published in English until 1887.

*An early photograph of Engels, which has been
asserted as showing him at age 20–25 (c. 1840–45)*

Engels continued his involvement with radical journalism and politics. He frequented areas popular among members of the English labour and Chartist movements, whom he met. He also wrote for several journals, including The Northern Star, Robert Owen's New Moral World and the Democratic Review.

Engels decided to return to Germany in 1844. On the way, he stopped in Paris to meet Marx. Marx had been living in Paris since late October 1843, after the Rheinische Zeitung was banned in March 1843 by Prussian governmental authorities. Prior to meeting Marx, Engels had become a fully developed materialist and 'scientific socialist', independently of Marx's philosophical development.

In Paris, Marx was publishing the Deutsch–Französische Jahrbücher with Arnold Ruge. Engels met Marx for a second time at the Café de la Régence on the Place du Palais in August 1844. The two quickly became close friends and remained so their entire lives. Marx had read and was impressed by The Condition, in which he had written "A class which bears all the disadvantages of the social order without enjoying its advantages … Who can demand that such a class respect this social order?" It was Engels's idea that the working class would lead the revolution against the bourgeoisie as society advanced toward socialism. Marx took this up as part of his own analysis.

Engels stayed in Paris to help Marx write The Holy Family, a critique of the Young Hegelians and the Bauer brothers, which was published in late February 1845. During this time in Paris, both Marx and Engels began their association with and then joined the secret revolutionary society called the League of the Just. The League of the Just had been formed in 1837 in France to promote an egalitarian society through the overthrow of the existing governments. In 1839, the League of the Just participated in the 1839 rebellion fomented by the French utopian revolutionary socialist, Louis Blanqui.

However, as Ruge remained a Young Hegelian in his belief, Marx and Ruge soon split and Ruge left the Deutsch–Französische Jahrbücher. Nonetheless, Marx remained friendly enough with Ruge so that he sent Ruge a warning in January 1845 that the Paris police were going to arrest him, Marx and others at the journal, requiring all to leave Paris within 24 hours. Marx himself was expelled from Paris by French authorities in February 1845 and settled in Brussels with his wife and one daughter. Engels returned to his home in Barmen, Germany, to work on his Condition, which was published in late May. But even before, Engels had moved to Brussels in late April to collaborate with Marx on another book, German Ideology. While living in Barmen, Engels began making contact with socialists in the Rhineland to raise money for Marx's publication efforts in Brussels. Marx and Engels began political organizing for the Social Democratic Workers' Party of Germany.

Belgium, founded only in 1830, was endowed with one of the most liberal constitutions in Europe and functioned as refuge for progressives from other countries. From 1845 to 1848, Engels and Marx lived in Brussels, spending much of their time organising the city's German workers. Shortly after their arrival, they contacted and joined the underground

German Communist League. The Communist League was the successor organisation to the old League of the Just which had recently disbanded. Influenced by Wilhelm Weitling, the Communist League was an international society of proletarian revolutionaries with branches in various European cities. Marx and Engels made many new important contacts through the Communist League. While most of the associates of Marx and Engels were German immigrants living in Brussels, some of their new associates were Belgians.

The Communist League commissioned Marx and Engels to write a pamphlet explaining the principles of communism. This became Manifesto of the Communist Party, better known as the Communist Manifesto. It

La Maison du Cygn (the Swan Tavern), Brussels, where the Communist Manifesto was written

was first published on 21 February 1848 and ends with the world-famous phrase: "Let the ruling classes tremble at a Communistic revolution. The proletariat have nothing to lose but their chains. They have a world to win ... Working Men of All Countries, Unite!"

There was a revolution in France in 1848 that soon spread to other Western European countries. These events caused Engels and Marx to return to their homeland of the Prussian Empire, specifically to the city of Cologne. While living in Cologne, they created and served as editors for a new daily newspaper called the Neue Rheinische Zeitung.

In 1849 Engels travelled to the Kingdom of Bavaria for the Baden and Palatinate revolutionary uprising, an even more dangerous involvement. Starting with an article called "The Magyar Struggle", written in January 1849, Engels, himself, began a series of reports on the Revolution and War for Independence of the newly founded Hungarian Republic.

However, during the June 1849 Prussian coup d'état the newspaper was suppressed. After the coup, Marx lost his Prussian citizenship, was deported, and fled to Paris and then London. Engels stayed in Prussia and took part in an armed uprising in South Germany as an aide-de-camp in the volunteer corps of August Willich. Engels also brought two cases of rifle cartridges with him when he went to join the uprising in Elberfeld in May 1849. When the uprising was crushed, Engels was one of the last members of Willich's volunteers to escape by crossing the Swiss border. Because of these military adventures, Marx's family in later years would call Engels 'the General'.

Engels travelled through Switzerland as a refugee and eventually made it to safety in England. On 6 June 1849 Prussian authorities issued an arrest warrant for Engels which contained a physical description as "height: 5 feet 6 inches; hair: blond; forehead: smooth; eyebrows: blond; eyes: blue; nose and mouth: well proportioned; beard: reddish; chin: oval; face: oval; complexion: healthy; figure: slender. Special characteristics: speaks very rapidly and is short-sighted." Once he was safe in Switzerland, Engels began to write down all his memories of the recent military campaign against the Prussians. This writing eventually became the article published under the name "The Campaign for the German Imperial Constitution."

Engels' family cotton mill in Salford, Manchester

Engels in Manchester

To help Marx with the new publishing effort in London, Engels sought ways to escape the continent and travel to London. He eventually arrived in November 1849. Once Engels made it to Britain, he decided to re-enter the Manchester company in which his father held shares, in order to be able to support Marx financially, so that Marx could work on Capital.

Engels didn't like his work in Manchester but did it for the good of the cause. Unlike his first period in England, Engels was now under police surveillance. He had "official" homes and "unofficial homes" all over Salford and other inner-city Manchester districts where he lived with Mary Burns under false names to confuse the police.

Despite his work at the mill, Engels found time to write a book on Martin Luther, the Protestant Reformation and the 1525 revolutionary war of the peasants, entitled The Peasant War in Germany. Engels also wrote a number of newspaper articles including "The Campaign for the German Imperial Constitution" which he finished in February

1850, and "On the Slogan of the Abolition of the State and the German 'Friends of Anarchy'" written in October 1850. In April 1851, he wrote the pamphlet "Conditions and Prospects of a War of the Holy Alliance against France".

Marx and Engels denounced French leader Louis Bonaparte when, in December 1851, he carried out a coup against the French government and made himself president for life. In condemning this action, Engels wrote to Marx, characterising the coup as occurring on "the 18th Brumaire", the date of Napoleon I's coup of 1799, according to the French Republican Calendar. Marx was later to incorporate this ironic characterisation of Louis Bonaparte's coup into his essay about the coup, calling the essay The Eighteenth Brumaire of Louis Bonaparte again using Engels's suggested characterisation. Marx also borrowed Engels' characterisation of Hegel's notion that history occurred twice, "once as a tragedy and secondly as a farce" in the first paragraph of his new essay.

Engels's house in Primrose Hill, London

In July 1851, Friedrich Engels's father arrived to visit him in Manchester. During the visit his father arranged for Friedrich to meet Peter Ermen who was to take over sole management of the office in Manchester. Engels started working as an office clerk, the same position he held in his teens while in Germany where his father's company was based. However, Friedrich worked his way up to become a partner of the firm by 1864. Five years later, Engels retired from the business and could focus more on his studies. During this time, Marx was living in London, but they were able to exchange ideas through daily correspondence.

Engels retires to London
In 1870, Engels moved to London where he and Marx lived until Marx's death in 1883. Engels' London home from 1870–1894 was at 122 Regent's Park Road. In October 1894 he moved to 41 Regent's Park Road, Primrose Hill, where he died the following year.

Mary Burns suddenly died of a heart disease in 1863, after which Engels became close with her younger sister Lydia ("Lizzie"). They lived openly as a couple in London and married in September 1878, hours before Lizzie's death.

After Marx's death, Engels devoted much of his remaining years to editing Marx's unfinished volumes of Capital, he also contributed significantly in other areas, including economics, as we shall see in the following chapters. Engels also made an argument using the anthropological evidence of the time to show that family structures changed over history, and that the concept of monogamous marriage came from the necessity within class society for men to control women to ensure their own children would inherit their property. He argued a future communist society would allow people to make decisions about their relationships free of economic constraints. One of the best examples of Engels' thoughts on these issues are in his work, The Origin of the Family, Private Property and the State.

Engels died of throat cancer (smoking?) in London on 5 August 1895, at the age of 74. Following cremation at Woking Crematorium, his ashes were scattered off Beachy Head, near Eastbourne as he had requested, with Eleanor Marx, Edward Aveling and Edouard Bernstein in attendance.

Engels in his mature years

The value of Engels

What value did Engels contribute to Marxian political economy? Marx himself gave us an evaluation. In Marx's 1859 preface to A Contribution to the Critique of Political Economy, Marx said: "Frederick Engels, with whom I maintained a constant exchange of ideas by correspondence since the publication of his brilliant essay on the critique of economic categories…arrived by another road (compare his Condition of the Working-Class in England) at the same result as I, and when in the spring of 1845 he too came to live in Brussels, we decided to set forth together our conception as opposed to the ideological one of German philosophy, in fact to settle accounts with our former philosophical conscience". A year later, Marx reaffirmed and indeed strengthened this claim in a letter in which he insisted that Engels "must" be considered "my alter ego."

As to Engels' intellectual abilities, Marx wrote in 1853 that "being a veritable walking encyclopaedia," Engels is "capable, drunk or sober, of working at any hour of the day or night, [he] is a fast writer and devilish quick in the uptake." However, Engels always recognised that Marx was at the heart of Marxism, or historical materialism.

A year after Marx's death he claimed to have been merely "second fiddle" to Marx: "My misfortune is that since we lost Marx I have been supposed to represent him. I have spent a lifetime doing what I was fitted for, namely playing second fiddle, and indeed I believe I acquitted myself reasonably well. And I was happy to have so splendid a first fiddle as Marx. But now that I am suddenly expected to take Marx's place in matters of theory and play first fiddle, there will inevitably be blunders and no one is more aware of that than I. And not until the times get somewhat more turbulent shall we really be aware of what we have lost in Marx. Not one of us possesses the breadth of vision that enabled him, at the very moment when rapid action was called for, invariably to hit upon the right solution and at once get to the heart of the matter. In more peaceful times it could happen that events proved me right and him wrong, but at a revolutionary juncture his judgement was virtually infallible."

Four years later in Ludwig Feuerbach and the End of Classical German Philosophy, Engels elaborated on this modest appreciation of his own contribution in print:

"Lately repeated reference has been made to my share in this theory, and so I can hardly avoid saying a few words here to settle this point. I cannot deny that both before and during my forty years' collaboration with Marx I had a certain independent share in laying the foundations of the theory, and more particularly in its elaboration. But the greater part of its leading basic principles, especially in the realm of economics and history, and, above all, their final trenchant formulation, belongs to Marx. What I contributed—at any rate with the exception of my work in a few special fields—Marx could very well have done without me. What Marx accomplished I would not have achieved. Marx stood higher, saw further, and took a wider and quicker view than all the rest of us. Marx was a genius; we others were at best talented. Without him the theory would not be by far what it is today. It therefore rightly bears his name."

On his death, Engels left a considerable estate, valued for probate at £25,265 equivalent to around £3 million in 2019. That's wealthy by most standards, but just one-tenth of what John Maynard Keynes left on his death. Keynes may have been worth more in money, but not in value.

Yet as biographer Gareth Stedman Jones has pointed out, Engels also made important original contributions to Marxism.[1]

"a number of basic and enduring Marxist propositions first surface in Engels' rather than Marx's early writings: the shifting focus from competition to production; the revolutionary novelty of modern industry marked by its crises of overproduction and its constant reproduction of a reserve army of labour; the embryo at least of the argument that the bourgeoisie produces its own gravediggers and that communism represents, not a philosophical principle, but "the real movement which abolishes the present state of things"; the historical delineation of the formation of the proletariat into a class; the differentiation between "proletarian socialism"; and small-master or lower-middle-class radicalism;

In his last years

and the characterisation of the state as an instrument of oppression in the hands of the ruling propertied class."

As for Marxian political economy, this book will show that Engels made even more contributions. The exchange value in an auction of Engels' works may be 50% of Marx's, but the use value of Engels' contribution is much higher than that.

CHAPTER TWO

Engels' critique of political economy

Marx to Engels: "As you know, I'm always late off the mark with everything, and I invariably follow in your footsteps" [2]

The first Marxist

At the age of just 22, Engels composed The Outlines of a Critique of Political Economy (the Umrisse), the first pioneering work of what we now call Marxian economics[3]. The Outlines was written to encourage Marx to concentrate on his own critique of political economy and capitalism. In composing the Umrisse, he had offered the first pioneering work of what we now call Marxian economics. Indeed, in this sense, Engels was a Marxist before Marx

Engel's critique is a brilliant analysis of the ideas of the contemporary economists, exposing their contradictions. And in the critique, he also begins to develop some of what became the basic categories of Marxist value and crisis theory well before Marx - if with some faults and limits.

The Umrisse provides a sophisticated evaluation of classical value theory and is a founding document in the Marxian theoretical tradition. First, Engels criticises David Ricardo for arguing that the market price of a commodity is set by the least efficient producer[4]. "Ricardo invariably supposes – which is theoretically false – that under all conditions in the market, it is the commodity produced in the most unfavourable circumstances which determines the market value."

And for first time in Marxian political economy, Engels refers to the anarchic and speculative nature of commodities trade: "whatever gives facilities to trade gives facilities to speculation. Trade and speculation are in some cases so nearly allied, that it is impossible to say at what precise point trade ends and speculation begins." He pinpoints the existence of trade cycles as endogenous to the emerging capitalist economy. Markets do not allocate resources and production efficiently because of inherent instability of both supply and demand. Only a planned society could ensure a rational allocation.

Preceding Marx, Engels argued that capitalism leads to the concentration and centralisation of property and the consequent demise of the middle class and the depression of wages to "the very barest necessities". And he notes that there is a bias under capitalism towards labour-displacing inventions which would create excessive unemployment, again seeding Marx's laws of general accumulation of capital and the reserve army of labour under capitalism.

Engels starts his critique with the fundamental weakness of classical political economy: its complete denial and/or ignorance of the role of private property in the capitalist economic system. Adam Smith, David Ricardo, Malthus and the later classical economists all start with the presumption that private property is a natural and eternal feature of any society. "It did not occur to economics to question the validity of private property. Therefore, the new economics was only half an advance. It was obliged to betray and to disavow its own premises, to have recourse to sophistry and hypocrisy so as to cover up the contradictions in which it became entangled."

Engels on value

And here Engels develops, for the first time, a Marxist theory of value. He starts by showing that the economists are divided and confused on the nature of value in the production and trade of commodities. The classical economists are at logger heads over the nature of value in production itself. Those like Ricardo and Smith reckon value is measured by the costs of production (as measured in labour time). On the other hand, Say reckons value depends of the 'utility' of what is produced. A commodity has no value if it is not useful and thus potentially in demand. On the other hand, its value surely must depend on the costs in labour time involved in producing it. So which is it? This debate has continued forever in mainstream economics, starting in the mid-19th century with the utility theorists of the neoclassical counter-revolution against the costs of production theorists of the classical school.[5]

Engel's answer presages Marx again. Engels argues that this is a false debate. Engels says the issue is resolved when it is realised that there is a double value in commodities. There is the real 'abstract' value, which Marx later called 'use-value' and there is the exchange value or price in the market. Under capitalism, commodities have both. "The economist who lives by antitheses has also of course a double value – abstract or real value and exchange-value. There was a protracted quarrel over the nature of real value between the English, who defined the costs of production as the expression of real value, and the Frenchman Say, who claimed to measure this value by the utility of an object. The quarrel hung in doubt from the beginning of the century, then became dormant without a decision having been reached. The economists cannot decide anything."

Engels takes us through the debate. "Let us try to introduce clarity into this confusion. The value of an object includes both factors, which the contending parties arbitrarily separate – and, as we have seen, unsuccessfully. Value is the relation of production costs to utility. The first application of value is the decision as to whether a thing ought to be produced at all i.e. as to whether utility counterbalances production costs. Only then can one talk of the application of value to exchange. The production costs of two objects being equal, the deciding factor determining their comparative value will be utility."

Only with the abolition of private property and markets would 'real value' be left on its own. "The contradiction between the real inherent utility of the thing and the determination of that utility, between the determination of utility and the freedom of those who exchange, cannot be superseded without superseding private property; and once this is superseded, there can no longer be any question of exchange as it exists at present."

> In the capitalist mode of production, competition in trade (markets) establishes an exchange value. He says: "the fundamental law of private property, that price is determined by the reciprocal action of production costs and competition. This purely empirical law was the first to be discovered by the economist; and from this law he then abstracted his "real value," i.e., the price at the time when competition is in a state of equilibrium, when demand and supply cover each other."
> But Engels' theory of value is not fully developed.

That was only achieved in Marx's Capital where Marx shows that value comes from the exploitation of labour to produce commodities that are realised on the market; and the concept of 'socially necessary labour time' becomes the basis of how both the supply-side of value (costs) are equalised with the demand-side (utility).

What is missing from Engels' account is Marx's theory of surplus value, that only labour creates value but by having a monopoly on the means of production, capitalists are able to appropriate the value created by labour. They turn labour itself into a commodity, labour power, and gain a surplus through the sale of the commodity for more value than the wages of labour. This discovery, as Engels always was quick to point out, was one of the major scientific achievements of Marx. In both accounts, it is clear that value (exchange value – Engels) only exists under capitalism where capital is separated from labour (Engels) and labour power is exploited and where surplus value is appropriated and realised in sale (Marx).

But again, Engels precedes Marx in his critique of Smith's three 'factors of production' that Smith puts forward as the basis of the capitalist 'macro economy'. There is land which accrues rent; capital that accrues profit or interest; and labour that receives wages. Engels recognises immediately that there are not three factors, but really just two: labour and land. That is because capital only exists because of private property. Without that there would be just human labour and nature.

"According to the economists, the production costs of a commodity consist of three elements: the rent for the piece of land required to produce the raw material; the capital with its profit, and the wages for the labour required for production and manufacture. But it becomes immediately evident that capital and labour are identical, since the economists themselves confess that capital is "stored-up labour." We are therefore left with only two sides – the natural, objective side, land; and the human, subjective side, labour, which includes capital. We have, then, two elements of production in operation – nature and man, with man again active physically and mentally, and can now return to the economist and his production costs."

Capital is really another form of labour which would not exist without private property. It is not a 'factor of production' but a social relation. The profit for capital comes from labour. And that profit is split into interest for the money lender and profit for the capitalist producer. "the economist separates capital from labour, and yet clings to the division without giving any other recognition to their unity than by his definition of capital as "stored-up labour." The split between capital and labour resulting from private property is nothing but the inner dichotomy of labour corresponding to this divided condition and arising out of it. And after this separation is accomplished, capital is divided once more into the original capital and profit – the increment of capital, which it receives in the process of production; although in practice profit is immediately lumped together with capital and set into motion with it. Indeed, even profit is in its turn split into interest and profit proper."

Engels on rent

In Umrisse, Engels develops the beginning of Marx's theory of absolute rent. Engels argues that it is the monopoly or private ownership of land that enables rent to be collected. There would be no rent without private property and monopoly. "If land could be had as easily as air, no one would pay rent. Since this is not the case, but since, rather, the extent of a piece of land to be appropriated is limited in any particular case, one pays rent for the appropriated, i.e., the monopolised land, or one pays down a purchase price for it."

He criticises Ricardo for ignoring this and just saying that rent is the income accrued from differing fertility in soil and farming returns. Yes, there are differential rents due to the productivity and technology employed on the land. In that sense, Ricardo was also right. "After the economist that the rent of land is the difference between the yield from the land for which rent is paid and from the worst land worth cultivating at all. As is well known, this is the definition of rent fully developed for the first time by Ricardo.... According to him, rent is the relation between the competition of those striving for the use of the land and the limited quantity of available land. Here at least is a return to the origin of rent."

But "rent is the relation between the productivity of the land, the natural side (which in turn consists of natural fertility and human cultivation – labour applied to effect improvement), and the human side, competition." As Marx said to Engels later: "Ricardo invariably supposes – which is theoretically false – that under all conditions in the market, it is the commodity produced in the most unfavourable circumstances which determines the market value. You yourself had already put forward the correct argument in Umrisse".[6]

Rent would not exist without private property, reminds Engels. "If here again we abandon private property, rent is reduced to its truth, to the rational notion which essentially lies at its root. The value of the land divorced from it as rent then reverts to the land itself. This value, to be measured by the productivity of equal areas of land subjected to equal applications of labour, is indeed taken into account as part of the production costs when determining the value of products."

Marx develops the theory of rent fully in Capital, where it is often ignored. Engels provides a simplified explanation in a preface to Capital, Volume 2. Engels says there: "Thus Adam Smith conceives surplus-value — that is, surplus-labour, the excess of labour performed and realised in the commodity over and above the paid labour, the labour which has received its equivalent in the wages — as the general category, of which profit in the strict sense and rent of land are merely branches." Engels quotes Marx: "he [Adam Smith] does not distinguish surplus-value as such as a category on its own, distinct from the specific forms it assumes in profit and rent. This is the source of much error and inadequacy in his inquiry, and of even more in the work of Ricardo." Thus, says Engels, "Marx's surplus-value, on the contrary, represents the *general form* of the sum of values appropriated without any equivalent by the owners of the means of production, and this form splits into the distinct, *converted* forms of profit and ground-rent in accordance with very peculiar laws which Marx was the first to discover."

Engels emphasises that " many intermediate links are required to arrive from an understanding of surplus-value in general at an understanding of its transformation into profit and ground-rent; in other words at an understanding of the laws of the distribution of surplus-value within the capitalist class. Ricardo goes considerably further than Adam Smith. He bases his conception of surplus-value on a new theory of value contained in embryo in Adam Smith, but generally forgotten when it comes to applying it."

As Engels says, "Marx shows that the value of the commodities remains the same, no matter what may be the proportion of these two parts, a law which he holds has but few exceptions. He even establishes a few fundamental laws, although couched in too general terms, on the mutual relations of wages and surplus-value (taken in the form of profit) and shows that ground-rent is a surplus over and above profit, which under certain circumstances does not accrue." For a modern analysis of Marx and Engels' theory of rent, see Basu.[7]

Engels on international trade

The issue for classical political economy at the time that Engels wrote Umrisse was whether economies would work better and fairer and in harmony if there was 'freedom of trade' and unleashed competition rather than the old system of monopolies and mercantile trade protections. The economists "affected a solemn abhorrence of the bloody terror of the Mercantile System and proclaimed trade to be a bond of friendship and union among nations as among individuals."

Engels says that the classical economists were right that mercantilism is an ideology and policy of greed that blocks productive cooperation and harmonious development. "Was Smith's system, then, not an advance? Of course, it was, and a necessary advance at that. It was necessary to overthrow the mercantile system with its monopolies and hindrances to trade, so that the true consequences of private property could come to light. It was necessary for all these petty, local and national considerations to recede into the background, so that the struggle of our time could become a universal human struggle.

But Engels points out neither did the alternative proposed: free trade. This was equally contradictory. "We gladly concede that it is only the justification and accomplishment of free trade that has enabled us to go beyond the economics of private property; but we must at the same time have the right to expose the utter theoretical and practical nullity of this free trade.. It will become evident that the protagonists of free trade are more inveterate monopolists than the old Mercantilists themselves."

That's because after proclaiming the end of the mercantile monopolists and "the pride of free trade", the classical economists continue to preserve the most important monopoly of all: private property. "Have we not overthrown the barbarism of the monopolies?" exclaim the hypocrites. "Have we not carried civilisation to distant parts of the world? Have we not brought about the fraternisation of the peoples, and reduced the number of wars?" Yes, all this you have done – but *how! You* have destroyed the small monopolies so that the *one* great basic monopoly, property, may function the more freely and unrestrictedly."

Contrary to the views of the classical economists, free trade and competition will not provide an equitable and harmonious development of production for all. While the classical economists offer competition and free trade against the evils of monopoly, they fail to recognise the biggest monopoly of all, the ownership of private property for the millionaires and the lack of it for the rest. This generates increased concentration of value production and increased centralisation of value appropriation: "under ordinary conditions, in accordance with the law of the stronger, large capital and large landed property swallow small capital and small landed property – i.e., centralisation of property.

In crises of trade and agriculture, this centralisation proceeds much more rapidly." while also generating more de-skilling and 'pauperisation' at the same time. "labour is weaker than either landed property or capital, for the worker must work to live, whilst the landowner can live on his rent, and the capitalist on his interest, or, if the need arises, on his capital or on capitalised property in land. The result is that only the very barest necessities, the mere means of subsistence, fall to the lot of labour; whilst the largest part of the products is shared between capital and landed property."

Competition leads to monopoly but in turn monopoly faces more competition in an unending spiral. "The opposite of competition is monopoly. Monopoly was the war-cry of the Mercantilists; competition the battle-cry of the liberal economists. It is easy to see that this antithesis is again a quite hollow antithesis. Every competitor cannot but desire to have the monopoly, be he worker, capitalist or landowner. Each smaller group of competitors cannot but desire to have the monopoly for itself against all others. Competition is based on self-interest, and self-interest in turn breeds monopoly. In short, competition passes over into monopoly. On the other hand, monopoly cannot stem the tide of competition – indeed, it itself breeds competition."

This is a powerful point to remember today against the theory of 'monopoly capitalism' and that capitalism fails because it breeds monopolies and not because of any inherent contradictions in its opposite, competitive capitalism.[8] Yes, monopoly (more accurately oligopoly) power has increased in the last 150 years since Marx and Engels forecast that the capitalist mode of production would lead to increased concentration and centralisation of capital. That shows that capitalism is in its late stage of development and so must be replaced by 'social monopoly'. But that also means that a return to competition would not work; either to renew the power of capitalist development or to reduce inequality.

The permanent damage to millions of people's lives in America, one of the richest capitalist economies in the world and the 'land of the free' is not the result of monopoly, but of the failure of capitalism to deliver enough things and services that people need, affordably. Yes, the rich elite sit atop their huge companies and banks 'earning' massive salaries and bonuses and hedge fund managers and bankers reap big capital gains. But the vast majority of Americans are struggling to make ends meet precisely because of 'competitive capitalism' and its failures.

Engels on cycles

A key point in Engels' Umrisse is the existence of regular and recurring crises in trade under capitalism. Instead of harmonious growth, competition leads to instability and cycles and worsening crises. This has been the case since the capitalist mode of production expanded and emerged in the industrial revolution 80 years earlier. Before capitalism, crises were the product of famine and disease; now they were the product of free trade for profit: "the economist comes along with his lovely theory of demand and supply, proves to you that "one can never produce too much," and practice replies with trade crises, which reappear as regularly as the comets, and of which we have now on the average one every five to seven years. For the last eighty years these trade crises have arrived just as regularly as the great plagues did in the past – and they have brought in their train more misery and more immorality than the latter."

But Engels retorts: "What are we to think of a law which can only assert itself through periodic upheavals? It is certainly a natural law based on the unconsciousness of the participants. If the producers as such knew how much the consumers required, if they were to organise production, if they were to share it out amongst themselves, then the fluctuations of competition and its tendency to crisis would be impossible. Carry on production consciously as human beings – not as dispersed atoms without consciousness of your species – and you have overcome all these artificial and untenable antitheses. But as long as you continue to produce in the present unconscious, thoughtless manner, at the mercy of chance – for just so long trade crises will remain; and each successive crisis is bound to become more universal and therefore worse than the preceding one. Then there is much superfluous productive power but the great mass of the nation has nothing to live on, so that the people starve from sheer abundance. For some considerable time, England has found herself in this crazy position, in this living absurdity. When production is subject to greater fluctuations, as it is bound to be in consequence of such a situation, then the alternation of boom and crisis, overproduction and slump, sets in. The economist has never been able to find an explanation for this mad situation."

Here for the first time, Engels refers to the anarchic and speculative nature of commodities trade: "whatever gives facilities to trade gives facilities to speculation. Trade and speculation are in some cases so nearly allied, that it is impossible to say at what precise point trade ends and speculation begins.". He also pinpointed the existence of trade cycles endogenous to the emerging capitalist economy. Markets do not allocate resources and production efficiently because of the inherent instability of both supply and demand. Only a planned society could ensure a rational allocation. "If we abandon private property, then all these unnatural divisions disappear. The difference between interest and profit disappears; capital is nothing without labour, without movement. The significance of profit is reduced to the weight which capital carries in the determination of the costs of production, and profit thus remains inherent in capital, in the same way as capital itself reverts to its original unity with labour."

Here Engels presages the arguments on crises found in the Manifesto of the Communist Party jointly written with Marx just four years later. Indeed, Engels' insights in his Umrisse are expressed in much the same words in the CM. These regular crises expose the irrationality of private property and trade, with a surplus of products in the market on the one hand and the unemployment of those producing them on the other.

Engels lays the cause of this irrationality on a system based on private property and competition (the category he takes from Smith). A fully worked out theory of crises under capitalism would come much later with Marx's work in his Grundrisse notes and Capital itself. But the essence of a theory of crises is already presented here in Engels' insights.

Subsequent modern research supports Engels.[9] During the early 19th century, GDP growth appears to have been relatively volatile. The Bank of England economists found that the gaps between major peaks and troughs were relatively short, at between two and three years implying a total cycle of around five years.

Agricultural output was a large contributor to the swings in output over this period, reflecting in part its 30% share of GDP. And to the extent that agricultural products were used as an input into other production processes, this may have had a further knock-on effect to the industrial sector.

A second reason was that Britain was at war for almost half of this period. The disruption to trade that accompanied these wars frequently led to weaker exports and economic downturns. But wars could also trigger cyclical upturns; concerns about potential disruptions to trade could lead to a near-term boost in activity.

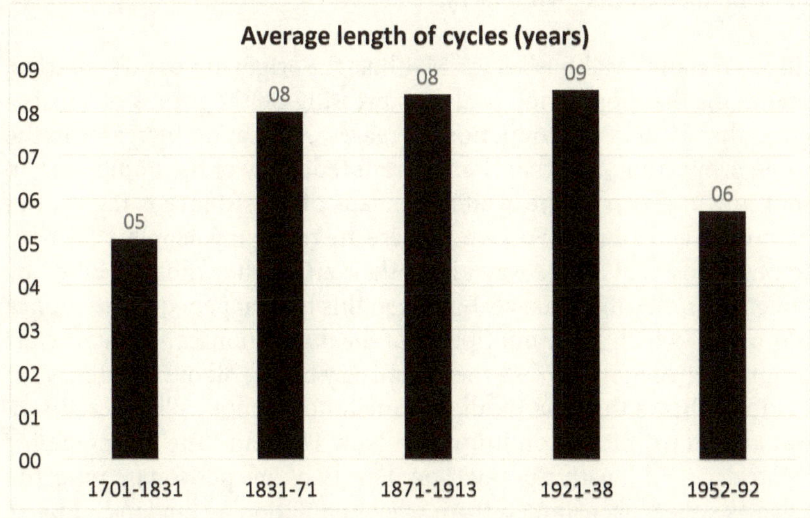

A third reason for the volatility of growth was the domestic investment cycle. Spending on the investment projects of the time — such as road (turnpike) and canal building — often fluctuated in response to waves of optimism (for example the canal 'mania' in the mid-1790s) as the industrialising economy of Britain developed.

During the second half of the period, financial crises increasingly began to involve the private sector more widely and often occurred at the peak of the economic cycle. Upturns in economic growth, although well founded, often encouraged speculative business activity much of which was financed by a network of trade credit. This financial structure depended heavily on confidence, which often vanished when the economy reached a turning point and expectations of growth were not fulfilled. The worst crises involved both the public and private sectors.

Engels on Malthus
Engels delivers a blistering dismissal of the ideas of the arch reactionary parson and economist, Thomas Malthus. Malthus is aware of recurring crises and slumps in capitalism. But unlike Smith, who hints that this due to too much competition or too much monopoly, Malthus reckons that it has nothing to do with capitalism or private property but due to nature, in particular, over population. The problem is that people just breed geometrically while production grows arithmetically. Labour is to be blamed for its own misery.

Engels recounts Malthus' view. "Malthus, the originator of this doctrine, maintains that population is always pressing on the means of subsistence; that as soon as production increases, population increases in the same proportion; and that the inherent tendency of the population to multiply in excess of the available means of subsistence is the root of all misery and all vice. For, when there are too many people, they have to be disposed of in one way or another: either they must be killed by violence or they must starve. But when this has happened, there is once more a gap which other multipliers of the population immediately start to fill up once more: and so the old misery begins all over again. What is more, this is the case in all circumstances – not only in civilised, but also in primitive conditions. In New Holland [The old name for Australia. - Ed.], with a population density of one per square mile, the savages suffer just as much from over-population as England." Engels ridicules Malthus's argument: "In short, if we want to be consistent, we must admit that the earth was already overpopulated when only one man existed."

And he goes on to describe the genocidal character of Malthus' conclusions. "The implications of this line of thought are that since it is precisely the poor who are the surplus, nothing should be done for them except to make their dying of starvation as easy as possible, and to convince them that it cannot be helped and that there is no other salvation for their whole class than keeping propagation down to the absolute minimum. Or if this proves impossible, then it is after all better to establish a state institution for the painless killing of the children of the poor, such as "Marcus" has suggested, whereby each working-class family would be allowed to have two and a half children, any excess being painlessly killed." Here Engels echoes the satire of Jonathan Swift's Modest Proposal, written one hundred years earlier, that suggested that the impoverished Irish might ease their economic troubles by selling their children as food to rich gentlemen and ladies.[10]

Engels adds that Malthus theory meant that "Charity is to be considered a crime, since it supports the augmentation of the surplus population. Indeed, it will be very advantageous to declare poverty a crime and to turn poor houses into prisons, as has already happened in England".

Engels concludes: "Am I to go on any longer elaborating this vile, infamous theory, this hideous blasphemy against nature and mankind? Am I to pursue its consequences any further? Here at last we have the immorality of the economist brought to its highest pitch. What are all the wars and horrors of the monopoly system compared with this theory! "

But he does go on to provide a powerful refutation of Malthus. Malthus is wrong because he ignores that powerful effect of the rising productivity of labour through science and mechanisation under capitalism that can easily keep pace with population growth. "For us the matter is easy to explain. The productive power at mankind's disposal is immeasurable. The productivity of the soil can be increased ad infinitum by the application of capital, labour and science." And so it has proved. The productivity of labour has rocketed since Malthus wrote, easily outstripping the expansion of the population; indeed, enabling such an expansion.

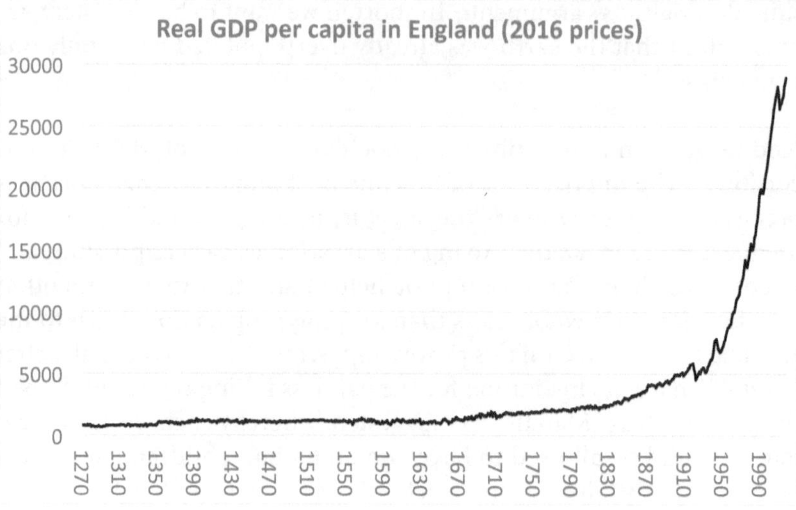

And anyway, it is not the population that matters but the size of employment. If all at working age were employed, production would meet the needs of all others too. And work would raise skills and productivity, Engels argues: "The second error he [Malthus] committed was to confuse means of subsistence with [means of] employment. That population is always pressing on the means of employment – that the number of people produced depends on the number of people who can be employed – in short, that the production of labour-power has been regulated so far by the law of competition and is therefore also exposed to periodic crises and fluctuations – this is a fact whose establishment constitutes Malthus' merit. But the means of employment are not the means of subsistence."

But as Engels also points out, in contrast to the techno-optimists, capitalism provides a contradiction: increased mechanisation can also mean the loss of jobs. Employment levels depend on the interests of private capital not on the rational development of the economy. Engels argues that capitalism leads to the concentration and "centralisation of property" and the consequent demise of the middle class and the depression of wages to "the very barest necessities" There is a bias under capitalism towards labour-displacing inventions which would create excessive population growth. Engels arguments again presage those of Marx's laws of general accumulation of capital and the reserve army of labour under capitalism to be found in Volume One of Capital.

Engels ends Umrisse by saying that: "In turning my attention to the effects of machinery, I am brought to another subject less directly relevant – the factory system; and I have neither the inclination nor the time to treat this here. Besides, I hope to have an early opportunity to expound in detail the despicable immorality of this system, and to expose mercilessly the economist's hypocrisy which here appears in all its brazenness."

Later Engels analyses the factory system of industrial capitalism in The Holy Family, written jointly with Marx,[11] and in his great work of labour economics, The Condition of the Working Class in England. (We come to these in the next chapter.)

Engels' Umrisse emphasises private property as the foundation of modern capitalist production; develops the nature of value under capitalism; outlines the continuing tension between competition and monopoly; free trade and protection; and offers an explanation of recurring and regular cycles of boom and slump in modern capitalism. All these are germs (and sometimes more than germs) of Marx's later critique in Capital and they are developed by Engels himself in his later works.

Marx himself recognised Engels' contribution in his introduction to Engels' pamphlet, Socialism: Utopian and Scientific (1880): "Frederick Engels, one of the foremost representatives of contemporary socialism, distinguished himself in 1844 with his Outlines of a Critique of Political Economy....The Outlines already formulates certain general principles of scientific socialism". [12]

There are limitations in Umrisse that Marx supersedes in his Critique. But Engels' contribution remains refreshingly modern and relevant, even if forgotten by most, including Marxist economists.

CHAPTER THREE

Engels on capital and labour

In his social and economic inquiry into the state of labour under the emerging industrial capital in mid-19th century England, The condition of the working class in England (hereafter called The Condition), Engels was the first to see that workers under capitalism were not slaves or serfs but worked as 'free labourers' for a wage.[13] But this was a certain peculiar freedom where workers were also selling a product on a market, a product of being a worker. In doing so, Engels developed a theory of wages under capitalism that Marx later adopted.

In the Condition, Engels proposed that there was an "historical and moral" element in the "degree of civilization" in the wage differences. Engels was also first to outline the theory of the "industrial reserve army", fully adopted by Marx in Capital. For Engels, the life situation of industrial workers fluctuated with the industrial crisis cycle and with surprisingly modern insight that the course of the industrial cycle is influenced by the fluctuations in world markets.

Engels reckoned that the long-term trend under capitalism would be a decrease in relative wages – in other words, the share of labour in GDP would decline, or in the language of Marx's Capital, there would be a rising rate of surplus value as a long-term trend.

While workers would fight to increase wages and their living standards through political and social movements, the industrial cycle and exploitation in capitalist accumulation meant that there was always a risk of falling back into poverty, homelessness, and even permanent unemployment.

Engels on wage labour
Marx said that Engels and he arrived at the same ideas on wages but by different roads. Engels had written The Condition in 1844 before he and Marx met up in Brussels in 1845 to publish a joint critique of German philosophy entitled The Holy Family.[14]

In The Condition, there are a range of "Marxian" theoretical issues, including the character of the industrialization process; the labour market, with particular reference to subsistence wages, the contrast between slave and "free" labour; the consequences of technical change; the reserve army of unemployed; and the nature of worsening crises.[15]

Engels had already developed left-wing ideas when he was despatched to England at the end of 1842 to work in the family firm of Ermen and Engels, manufacturers of sewing thread in Manchester. He arrived in England only weeks after the Chartist general strike of 1842 which, despite its eventual failure, had demonstrated the potential power of the workers. The strike's centre was in Manchester and the surrounding areas of Lancashire and Cheshire, the areas of textile production. England was by far the most advanced industrial economy in the world. It was already leading the world in the production of cotton, coal and iron. Its working class was also the most advanced in the world, organised through the Chartist movement.

Engels was horrified at the poverty and misery that he saw in Manchester.

A Manchester cotton factory

The city had grown up around the cotton industry and was a mass of filthy slums. Infant mortality, epidemic diseases and overcrowding were all facts of life. Up to a quarter of the city's population were immigrant Irish, driven there by even worse conditions in their own country. Poverty had existed in the old towns and rural areas – as it had done in Germany – but the growth of the big cities exacerbated and accentuated these conditions.

Engels travelled round, spoke to workers and studied official statistics to produce The Condition. It documents not only how people lived, but also explains how this state of affairs could be – and needed to be – changed. The new working class soon accounted for the mass of the population, as capitalist methods of manufacturing destroyed many of the old artisan or middle classes, turning the bulk of them or their children into workers. The needs of manufacturing industry led to the building of factories and mills and, moreover, 'population becomes centralised just as capital does. Industrial towns then developed into the great cities that Engels observed when he first visited England. He describes in great detail the condition of life in these cities, using a variety of contemporary press reports, official investigations and even diagrams of the back-to-back houses which formed the early Manchester slums. Nothing escapes Engels' eye, not even the workers' diet:

> The better paid workers, especially those in whose families every member is able to earn something, have good food as long as this state of things lasts; meat daily and bacon and cheese for supper. Where wages are less, meat is used only two or three times a week, and the proportion of bread and potatoes increases. Descending gradually, we find the animal food reduced to a small piece of bacon cut up with the potatoes; lower still, even this disappears, and there remain only bread, cheese, porridge and potatoes, until on the lowest round of the ladder, among the Irish, potatoes form the sole food ... But all this pre-supposes that the workman has work. When he has none, he is wholly at the mercy of accident, and eats what is given him, what he can beg or steal. And, if he gets nothing, he simply starves.[16]

Engels summed up the position of the poorest. "In 1842 England and Wales counted 1,430,000 paupers, of whom 222,000 were incarcerated in workhouses – Poor Law Bastilles the common people call them. – thanks to the humanity of the Whigs! Scotland has no poor law, but poor people in plenty. Ireland, incidentally, can boast of the gigantic number of 2,300,000 paupers."

Slavery was awful, but, in England, after the1833 abolition of slavery bill, the poor in England were still being sold in markets. Parents selling their children because they had no homes and couldn't feed them. In the mines in Lancashire 5 year old children spent 12 hrs a day, completely alone in complete darkness, wafting the fans. The average life expectancy in Howarth, when the Brontes lived there, was 25. Even after the great reform bill only 6% of Britons had the right to vote. I fear that the poor in Britain were treated just as badly as many slaves."

Things were different for the rich, but were they happy? "This successful industry of England, with its plethoric wealth, has as yet made nobody rich; it is an enchanted wealth, and belongs yet to nobody. [...] We can spend thousands where we once spent hundreds; but can purchase nothing good with them. [...] Many men eat finer cookery, drink dearer liquors, [...] what increase of blessedness is there? Are they better, beautifuller, stronger, braver? Are they even what they call 'happier'?"

In his Condition, Engels quoted the liberal Carlyle on the class nature of England in the 1840s: "An idle landowning aristocracy which "have not yet learned even to sit still and do no mischief", a working aristocracy submerged in Mammonism, who, when they ought to be collectively the leaders of labour, "captains of industry", are just a gang of industrial buccaneers and pirates. A Parliament elected by bribery, a philosophy of simply looking on, of doing nothing, of laissezfaire, a wornout, crumbling religion, a total disappearance of all general human interests, a universal despair of truth and humanity, and in consequence a universal isolation of men in their own "brute individuality", a chaotic, savage confusion of all aspects of life, a war of all against all, a general death of the spirit, a dearth of "soul", that is, of truly human consciousness: a disproportionately strong working class, in intolerable oppression and wretchedness, in furious discontent and rebellion against the old social order, and hence a threatening, irresistibly advancing democracy – everywhere chaos, disorder, anarchy, dissolution of the old ties of society, everywhere intellectual insipidity, frivolity, and debility. – that is the condition of England."

In the Holy Family, written jointly with Marx (Engels wrote it and then Marx expanded it), Engels attacks the views of Otto Bauer's Criticism[17]. Bauer argued that the working class had nothing to fear from the industrial revolution and the replacement of labour by machinery. Engels points out that workers did not agree with Bauer and pushed hard for a reduction in hours "the English workers — who in April and May held meeting after meeting, drew up petition after petition, and all for the Ten Hour Bill, and displayed more agitation throughout the factory districts than at any time during the past two years - it is evident that "legislation limiting the working day has also occupied their attention".

Engels guffawed at Bauer's optimistic naivety. "In reality all grades of wages exist in English factories, from Is 6d to 40s and more; but according to Criticism only one rate is paid — 11s! In reality the machine replaces manual labour; but according to Criticism it replaces thought. In reality, the association of workers for wage rises is allowed in England, but according to Criticism it is prohibited. In reality, factory labour is extremely tiring and gives rise to specific diseases — there are even special medical works on them. But according to Criticism "excessive exertion cannot be a hindrance to work, for the power is provided by the machine". In reality, the machine is a machine;

Dark satanic mills

for as it does not rest, neither can the worker, and he is subordinated to an alien will."

Engels on labour

But Engels' book is much more than reportage of the terrible conditions in which workers lived. Woven into it is the political analysis of capitalism which Marx and Engels later developed but which even at this stage was central to the book's analysis. Engels starts by looking at how the Industrial Revolution transformed the old ways of working to such an extent that it created a whole class of wage labourers, the proletariat. The introduction of machinery into the production of textiles, coal and iron turned the British economy into the most dynamic in the world, creating a mass of communications networks – iron bridges, railways, canals – which in turn led to more industrial development.

The most important effect of the 18th century for England was the creation of the proletariat by the industrial revolution. The new industry demanded a constantly available mass of workers for the countless new branches of production, and moreover workers such as had previously not existed. Up to 1780 England had few proletarians, a fact which emerges inevitably from the social condition of the nation as described above. Industry concentrated work in factories and towns; it became impossible to combine manufacturing and agricultural activity, and the new working class was reduced to complete dependence on its labour. What had hitherto been the exception became the rule and spread gradually outside the towns too. Small-scale farming was ousted by the large tenant farmers and thus a new class of agricultural labourers was created. The population of the towns trebled and quadrupled and almost the whole of this increase consisted solely of workers. The expansion of mining likewise required a large number of new workers, and those too lived solely from their daily wage.

At the heart of the misery Engels describes is the very nature of the capitalist system. The competition between capitalists leads them to pay their workers as little as possible, while trying to squeeze more and more work from them: 'If a manufacturer can force the nine hands to work an extra hour daily for the same wages by threatening to discharge them at a time when the demand for hands is not very great, he discharges the tenth and saves so much wages. This leads in turn to competition between workers for jobs, and to the creation of a pool of unemployed who can be pulled into the workforce when business is booming and laid off again when it is slack. The existence of this reserve of unskilled and unemployed workers – especially among the immigrant Irish in the cities of the 1840s – holds down the level of wages and conditions for all workers."

Engels on wages

In 1842 the Chartists had demanded a People's Charter. But Engels commented "Social evils cannot be cured by People's Charters…Social evils need to be studied and understood, and this the mass of the workers has not yet done up till now."

So Engels developed a theory of wages. He argued that a drop in the price of bread must be followed by a drop in wages, so that all would remain as it was". Furthermore, "these people expect that, granted there is a drop in wages and a consequent lowering of production costs, the result will be an expansion of the market. This, they expect, would lead to a reduction of competition among the workers, and consequently wages would still be kept a little higher in comparison with the price of bread than they are now."

It was the intraclass competition between workers that was "the sharpest weapon against the proletariat in the hands of the bourgeoisie," which explains "the effort of the workers to nullify this competition by associations." In the absence of union counterpressure, the advantage is with the employing class, which "has gained a monopoly of all means of existence," and "which is protected in its monopoly by the power of the state."

In his pamphlet, the Principles of Communism of 1847, a work often neglected by those who have read the Communist Manifesto written later, Engels argued that because labour is a "commodity" like any other, it is subject to "all the fluctuations of the market," but on an average equal to its "cost of production", namely the subsistence level to survive and reproduce. "The average price of wage-labour is the minimum wage, i.e., that quantum of the means of subsistence, which is absolutely requisite to keep the labourer in bare existence as a labourer. What, therefore, the wage labourer appropriates by means of his labour, merely suffices to prolong and reproduce a bare existence."

Downward pressure on the subsistence minimum itself is a result of deskilling and consequential replacement of men by women and children: "the more modern industry becomes developed, the more is the labour of men superseded by that of women and children… Differences of age and sex have no longer any distinctive social validity for the working class. All are instruments of labour, more or less expensive to use, according to their age and sex."

There is downward pressure on the real wage resulting from the use of machinery and division of labour, and from downward mobility into the workforce in consequence of the concentration of capital: "The former lower strata of the middleclass – the small tradespeople, shopkeepers, the retired, the handicraftsmen and peasants – all these sink gradually into the proletariat, partly because their diminutive capital does not suffice for the scale on which modern industry is carried on, and is swamped in the competition with the large capitalists, partly because their specialized skill is rendered worthless by new methods of production".

Engels gives a fairly complete and detailed description of the English factory legislation from 1802 to 1844 - with the struggle of the labour movement for the legal limitation of the working day as a guide. Engels praises the work of the factory inspectors whose reports he uses. Indeed,

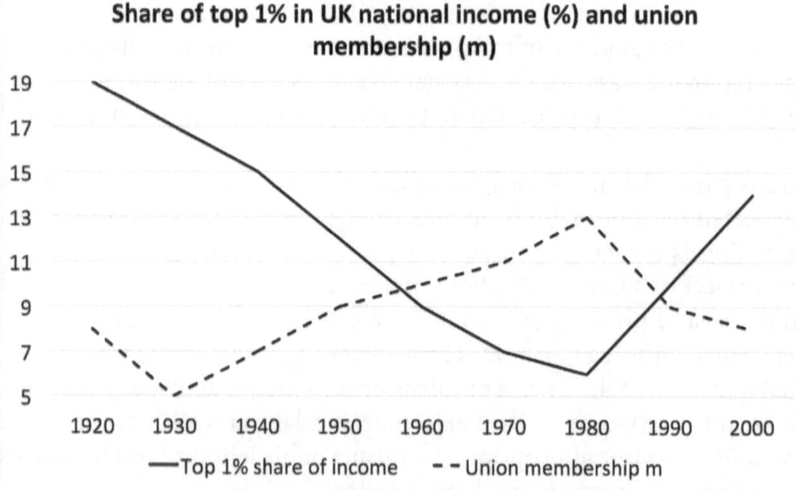

Engels admits that the factory laws, thanks to the work of the inspectors, curbed some of the worst excesses in child labour, night work, women's work. But liberal legislation could not help working people; they must help themselves. Unionisation was essential.

That unionisation helps to sustain real wage levels and the share of labour in output has since been borne out by many studies. Where trade union membership has fallen and union influence decreased in workplaces, income inequalities have risen. At the same time, wealth has become concentrated more and more in the hands of the richest 1% in society.

Conversely, during periods when union membership has grown and in countries where unions were strong, pay inequality has declined. In the UK, between 1937 and 1979, trade union membership more than doubled (increasing by 126%), while the share of income going to the top 1% fell by two-thirds (65%). However, between 1979 and 2014, a period during which membership of unions fell by half (47%) in the UK, the share of wealth that went to the richest 1% more than doubled (leaping by 134%).[18]

Across the 37 member countries of the OECD, where collective bargaining was more common in workplaces, inequality tended to be lower. "In recent years, we have seen union membership fall by half, and collective bargaining coverage fall by two-thirds. At the same time, inequality has rocketed. Over the past four decades, the share of income going to the top 1% has nearly tripled." (OECD).[19]

For most of the last 40 years, pay in the US has stagnated for all but the highest paid workers and inequality has risen dramatically. The share of workers covered by a collective bargaining agreement dropped from 27 percent to 11.6 percent between 1979 and 2019, meaning the union coverage rate is now less than half where it was 40 years ago.[20] De-unionization accounts for a sizable share of the growth in inequality over that period—around 13–20 percent for women and 33–37 percent for men. Applying these shares to annual earnings data reveals that working people are now losing on the order of $200 billion per year as a result of the erosion of union coverage over the last four decades—with that money being redistributed upward, to the rich.[21]

Ahead of Marx, Engels began to explain how workers were exploited despite receiving a 'fair day's pay for a fair day's work'. As Engels put it: "The bourgeoisie "offers [the proletarian] the means of living, but only for an 'equivalent,' for his work," and it "even lets him have the appearance of acting from free choice, of making a contract with free, unconstrained consent, as a responsible agent who has attained his majority," though he is "in law and in fact, the slave of the bourgeoisie." Thus "the worker of today seems to be free because he is not sold once for all, but piecemeal by the day, the week, the year, and because no one owner sells him to another, but he is forced to sell himself in this way instead, being the slave of no particular person, but of the whole property-holding class". Later Marx would fully develop this notion into the category of "labour power" as the object of purchase by employers.

But the "subsistence" wage is the worker's bottom price: "To...competition of the workers there is but one limit; no worker will work for less than he needs to subsist. If he must starve, he will prefer to starve in idleness than in toil"(376).But this minimum is not purely physiological, but socially determined; "the Englishman, who is still somewhat civilised, needs more than the Irishman, who goes in rags, eats potatoes, and sleeps in a pig-sty." Again, Engels presents the 'social aspect' of the value of labour power that Marx was to develop later in Capital.

In sum, Engels argued that the average rate of wages is equal to the sum of necessaries sufficient to keep up the race of 'workmen' in a certain country according to the standard of life habitual in that country. For Engels, there was great merit in trade unions because they struggled to keep up the rate of wages and to reduce working hours and thus tended to keep up and to raise the standard of life. Engels identified the trade union differential – so visible in neo-liberal 20th century capitalism. A powerful trade union enables the one set of workers to maintain a comparatively high standard of life; while the non-union workers are disorganised and powerless and their standard of life is lower.

Engels on machinery

Another brilliant concept by Engels was to anticipate Marx's general law of accumulation and its dual nature. On the one hand, the introduction of new machinery or technology will lead to the loss of jobs for those workers using outdated technology. On the other hand, the new industries and techniques could create new jobs.

Again, this debate over the impact of technology and jobs is topical with the advent of robots and artificial intelligence now. Robots do not do away with the contradictions within capitalist accumulation. The essence of capitalist accumulation is that to increase profits and accumulate more capital, capitalists want to introduce machines that can boost the productivity of each employee and reduce costs compared to competitors. This is the great revolutionary role of capitalism in developing the productive forces available to society.

But there is a contradiction. In trying to raise the productivity of labour with the introduction of technology, there is process of labour shedding. New technology replaces labour. Yes, increased productivity might lead to increased production and open up new sectors for employment to compensate. But over time, a capital-bias or labour shedding means less new value is created (as labour is the only form of value) relative to the cost of invested capital. There is a tendency for profitability to fall as productivity rises. In turn, that leads eventually to a crisis in production that halts or even reverses the gain in production from the new technology. This is solely because investment and production depend on the profitability of capital in our modern mode of production.

Now mainstream economics has noticed that this is not good news for labour and that 'capital bias' in technology could explain the falling labour share and growing inequalities. As modern Keynesian Paul Krugman put it: "The effect of technological progress on wages depends on the bias of the progress; if it's capital-biased, workers won't share fully in productivity gains, and if it's strongly enough capital-biased, they can actually be made worse off. So it's wrong to assume, as many people on the right seem to, that gains from technology always trickle down to workers; not necessarily. It's also wrong to assume, as some (but not all) on the left sometimes seem to that rapid productivity growth is necessarily jobs- or wage-destroying. It all depends."[22]

So as Engels first suggested in the Condition, it does depend on the class struggle between labour and capital over the appropriation of the value created by the productivity of labour. And clearly labour has been losing that battle, particularly in recent decades, under the pressure of anti-trade union laws, ending of employment protection and tenure, the reduction of benefits, a growing reserve army of unemployed and underemployed and through the globalisation of manufacturing.

Engels describes domestic spinning and weaving under conditions of "constant increase in the demand for the home market keeping pace with the slow increase of population". The "victory of machine-work over hand-work" – reflecting the competitive advantage of the new technologies – entailed "a rapid fall in price of all manufactured commodities, prosperity of commerce and manufacture, the conquest of nearly all the unprotected foreign markets, the sudden multiplication of capital and national wealth"; and also "a still more rapid multiplication of the proletariat" and "the destruction of all property-holding and of all security of employment for the working-class". So industrialisation and the introduction of machinery destroys small businesses and self-employment and drives people into large workplaces where jobs appear as companies with better technology and lower costs can gain market share at home and abroad.

Engels quotes Adam Smith: "[t]hat the demand for men, like that for any other commodity, necessarily regulates the production of men, quickens it when it goes on too slowly, and stops it when it advances too fast" (Engels's emphasis). Thus "the workers previously employed in producing them are therefore driven out of work, and are also removed from the market, and so it goes on, always the same old round"[23]

Empirical evidence supports Engels' thesis. Carl Frey reckons that the early inventions of the Industrial Revolution were predominantly labour-replacing: "If technology replaces labor in existing tasks, wages and the share of national income accruing to labor may fall. If, in contrast, technological change is augmenting labor, it will make workers more productive in existing tasks or create entirely new labour-intensive activities, thereby increasing the demand for labour."[24]

The divergence between output and wages, in other words, is consistent with this being a period where technology was primarily replacing labour. Artisan workers in the domestic system were replaced by machines, often tended by children—who had very little bargaining power and often worked without wages. The growing capital share of income meant that the gains from technological progress were very unequally distributed: corporate profits were captured by industrialists, who reinvested them in factories and machines." There was a growing gap between wages and productivity growth as workers were displaced by new technology and nominal wages were kept stagnant,

Engels' 'pause'

Was Engels (and the workers he talked to) right about the growth in real wages in 1840s Britain? Economic historians since, on the whole, agree. Robert Allen has characterised the period, particularly after the end of the Napoleonic Wars up to the time that Engels arrived in Manchester as the 'Engels pause'.[25]

As per capita gross domestic product grew, real wages of the British working class remained relatively constant. Capitalists and financiers of new, large-scale manufacturing businesses accumulated the gains from economic development, using them to expand their industries. Charles Feinstein found that working-class wages during that same period increased by 12%, a noticeably slower and comparatively stagnant rate.[26]

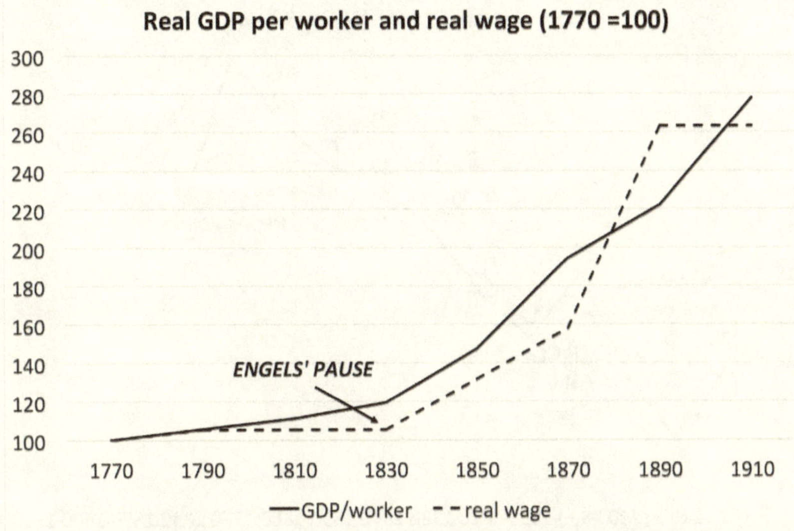

The two main studies show that real wages (after inflation) were more or less flat from 1805-1820, a period of economic depression in England. There was a pick-up in the 1830s. But the 'hungry forties' as they were called, saw a significant fall in real wages, mainly because of rising food prices that were not expunged until the abolition of the Corn Laws in 1846. During the forties there were two slumps, 1841 and 1847, with Engels' study straddling both. By 1847, real wages had been stagnant (at best) for over ten years.[27]

HM Boot looked at the wages of one the largest British companies, the East India Company. He found that clerical workers doubled their wages compared to manual workers during the industrial revolution to the point.

 when Engels arrived in England.[28] "After 1825 income improvements decidedly shifted in favour of those sections of the middle class dependent on the growth of commerce and finance" Things have not changed in the 21st century.

Allen argued that the British economy from 1760 to 1913 passed through a two stage evolution of inequality. In the first half of the 19th century,

the real wage stagnated while output per worker expanded. The profit rate doubled and the share of profits in national income expanded at the expense of labour and land. Technical progress was the prime mover behind the industrial revolution. Capital accumulation was a necessary complement. The surge in inequality was intrinsic to the growth process: technical change increased the demand for capital and raised the profit rate and capital's share. The rise in profits, in turn, sustained the industrial revolution by financing the necessary capital accumulation. After the middle of the 19th century, accumulation had caught up with the requirements of technology and wages rose in line with productivity.

More recently, the Bank of England confirmed that Engels was right about real wages and productivity in the 1840s. There was an Engels'pause.

Indeed, former Bank of England governor Mark Carney recently suggested that the period since the Great Recession of 2008-9 has repeated Engels' pause. Carney pointed out that since the global financial crash of 2008, average real incomes in Britain have taken the biggest plunge since the 1860s, when "Karl Marx was scribbling in the British Library." And "it was the poorest (who) are hit the hardest. During recessions, the lower-skilled, lower paid people tend to lose their jobs first."[29]

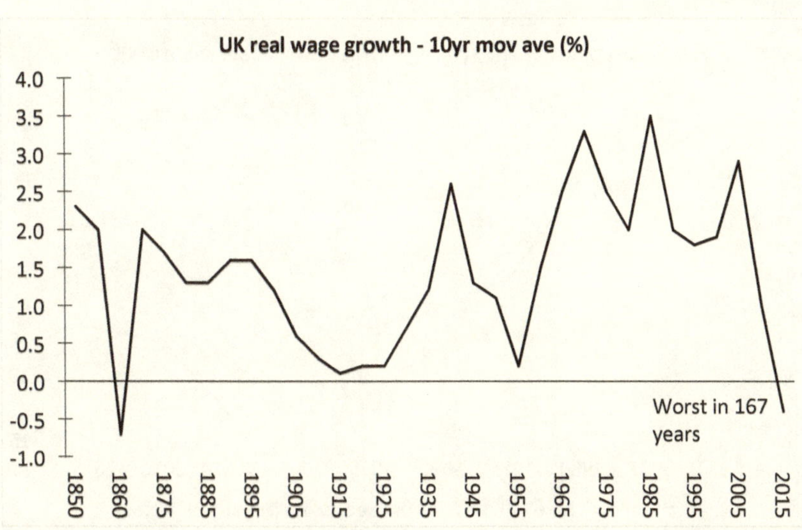

Carney continued that "Engels exposed the misery and poverty engendered by the replacement of manual skills with machines and kept real incomes stagnant." Now, says Carney, "Marxism might again be relevant with a new burst of 'capital bias' (ie a rise in machines relative to human labour power). Automation may not just destroy millions of jobs. For all except a privileged minority of high-tech workers, the collapse in the demand for labour could hold down living standards for decades. In such a climate, "Marx and Engels may again become relevant" said Carney.

Carney was reiterating Engels' insights and Marx's general law of capitalist accumulation that capitalist accumulation will expand and promote machines to replace human labour. But this will not lead automatically to higher living standards, less toil and more freedom for the individual, but mostly to downward pressure on real incomes, not only of those losing their jobs to machines, but in general. It would also lead to more not less toil for those with jobs, while leaving millions in a state of 'precarious labour' – a reserve army for capital to exploit or dispense with as the cycle of accumulation demands.

However, Carney was at pains to claim that capitalism has worked for people: "global markets and technological progress has lifted more than

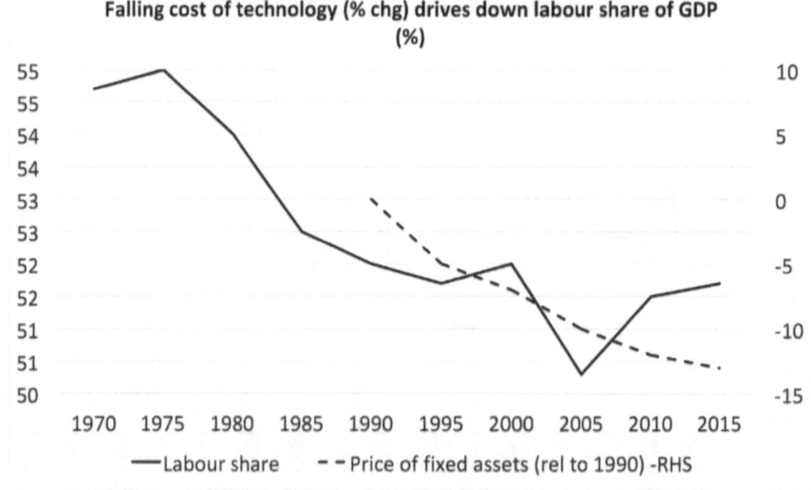

a billion people out of poverty, while a series of technological advances have fundamentally enriched our lives". And Engels too looked at this other side of the coin. He argued that there are "other circumstances" at play including re-employment generated by the reduced costs resulting from new technology: "The introduction of the industrial forces already referred to for increasing production leads, in the course of time, to a reduction of prices of the articles produced and to consequent increased consumption, so that a large part of the displaced workers finally, after long suffering, find work again in new branches of labour."

Engels' theory again rejected the Malthusian explanation. Population growth is a response to growing employment opportunities, not vice versa: "The bourgeois forgets, in fighting the working-man, the most ordinary principles of his own Political Economy. He, who at other times swears by Malthus, cries out in his anxiety before the workers: 'Where could the millions by which the population of England has increased find work, without the improvements in machinery?' As though the bourgeois did not know well enough that without machinery and the expansion of industry which it produced, these 'millions' would never have been brought into the world and grown up!"

But Engels' argument was not an apology for capitalism, because new jobs don't last: "as soon as the operative has succeeded in making himself at home in a new branch, if he actually does succeed in so doing, this, too, is taken from him, and with it the last remnant of security which remained to him for winning his bread."

And it is really only in sectors of industry that require high skill and/ or are subject to union protection that increasing wages and jobs are sustained: "The so-called fine spinners...do receive high wages, thirty to forty shillings a week, because they have a powerful association for keeping wages up, and their craft requires long training; but the coarse spinners who have to compete against self-actors (which are not as yet adapted for fine spinning), and whose association was broken down by the introduction of these machines, receive very low wages"

Generally, however, "that wages in general have been reduced by the improvement of machinery is the unanimous testimony of the operatives. The bourgeois assertion that the condition of the working-class has been improved by machinery is most vigorously proclaimed a falsehood in every meeting of working-men in the factory districts."

Engels reckoned that falling wages, primarily affecting unskilled occupations but carried over somewhat to the labouring class as a whole was also affected by (Irish) immigration: "it is easy to understand how the degrading position of the English workers, engendered by our modern industry and its immediate consequences, has been still more degraded by the presence of Irish competition." The main cause of low wages is the power of employers over non-unionised workers, the threat of machinery and the industrial cycle under capitalism. But immigration of cheap labour can add to that.

This issue remains just as topical now with evidence for and against.[30] Modern research for the UK points to no convincingly large negative effects of immigration on average wages of British-born workers. This is largely in line with studies done in other countries. Some studies have pointed to the possibility of effects on the distribution of wages, holding wage growth back at the lower end and pushing wages up at the higher end. However the negative effects are small.

In sum, Engels concludes that wage levels are determined by the vagaries of capitalist competition, capital's control of technology and means of production and the struggle between labour and employers. What decides the value of labour power and wages is the balance of the competitive struggle between the workers and the employers – but also, over the longer term, the productivity of labour.

Engels and the reserve army of labour
In the Condition, Engels presents for the first time what was to become one of Marx's main concepts in his law of accumulation: the reserve army of labour, by referring to "an unemployed reserve army of workers." Engels says: "English manufacture must have, at all times save the brief periods of highest prosperity, an unemployed reserve army of workers, in order to be able to produce the masses of goods required by the market in the liveliest months. This reserve army is larger or smaller, according as the state of the market occasions the employment of a larger or smaller proportion of its members....This reserve army...is the "surplus population" of England, which keeps body and

soul together by begging, stealing, street-sweeping, collecting manure, pushing hand-carts, driving donkeys, peddling, or performing occasional small jobs." Engels provides empirical support to this thesis. "Of this surplus population there are, according to the reports of the Poor Law commissioners, on an average, a million and a half in England and Wales...."

But Engels points out that these 'official' figures for unemployment are an underestimate because "this million and a half includes only those who actually apply to the parish for relief; the great multitude who struggle on without recourse to this most hated expedient, it does not embrace." We could repeat this criticism of modern official unemployment data, which often fails to account for workers not claiming benefit but wanting employment.

Population growth may fuel the secular expansion of the work force, which sometimes is fully employed at cyclical peaks and in excess supply to a greater or lesser extent at other periods of the cycle. Indeed, Engels noted in a preface to his later edition of the Condition, that, during industrial crises, the reserve army rises sharply: "During a crisis this number [surplus population] naturally increases markedly and want

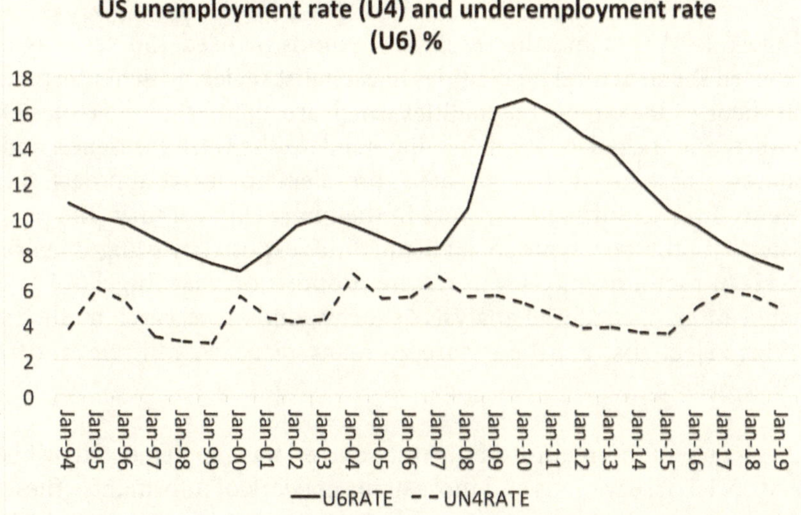

reaches its highest pitch. Take, for instance, the crisis of 1842, which, being the latest, was the most violent; for the intensity of the crisis increases with each repetition, and the next, which may be expected not later than 1847 ("And it came in 1847" Engels comments in hindsight) and will probably be still more violent and lasting".

Engels returns to his theory of value expounded in Umrisse (see chapter 2), namely that market prices, including the price of labour, are inherently volatile due to competition. There is no tendency to equilibrium under capitalism: "market price" – is "determined by the reciprocal action of costs and competition" and, indeed, that price in "a state of equilibrium, when demand and supply cover each other," reflects "real value" or costs (p. 30). However, such "equilibrium" was at best only momentary and it was objectionable to base oneself on such abstractions. Thus, from the beginning, Marxian political economy (before Marx!) rejected general equilibrium analysis for a dynamic non-equilibrium model ie laws of motion in capitalism.

Engels looks back
"According to my own opinions and authentic sources" Engels, in his Preface to the First German Edition of The Condition of the Working Class in England, says that he preferred to use sources which originated from the bourgeoisie and cast 'their own words in their teeth'

Engels' 1845 text and the research methods he used 150 years ago, exposed the structural inequalities in capitalist society which informed his theory, for example inequalities which are manifest in the issues of poverty and the polarization of living standards between the richest and poorest. These social problems are as prevalent now as we approach the twenty-first century as they were in the nineteenth century. The persistence of the very same social inequalities exposed by using Engels's 1842-44 methodology supports the proposition that Engels's 1845 publication, his material analysis of society and his research methods which reject abstract theory are, in many respects, still relevant in 1990s Britain.

Engels's use of the 'requisite authentic sources' was supplemented by his own social observations and those of his network of informants. These observations revealed the reality of the material conditions under which the working class in England lived. There are numerous biographies and texts which support the argument that Engels's network was of particular importance to his 1845 publication.

In his later article "England 1845 to 1885", Engels tried to illustrate the changes in the situation of the working class in the years since the Condition had been written. In this article, Engels describes the temporary improvements in the situation of the working class. There was a "permanent uplift" only for the factory workers and for unionized workers, but not for the "big crowd" of other workers, not even during the long expansion of trade and industry after the 1848 revolutions were defeated.

In the long boom of the 1850s and 1860s, for England, the effects of this domination of the manufacturing capitalists were at first sight startling. Trade revived and extended to a degree unheard of even in this cradle of modern industry; the previous astounding creations of steam and machinery dwindled into nothing compared with the immense mass of productions of the twenty years from 1850 to 1870, with the overwhelming figures of exports, and imports, of wealth accumulated in the hands of capitalists and of human working power concentrated in the large towns.

Even so, progress was interrupted, as before, by a crisis every ten years; in 1857 as well as in 1868; but as Engels remarked, "these revulsions were now considered as natural, inevitable events which must be fatalistically submitted to, and which always set themselves right in the end."

And what about the condition of the working class during this period? There was temporary improvement even for the great mass. But this improvement always was reduced to the old level by the influx of the great body of the unemployed reserve, by the constant superseding of hands by new machinery, by the immigration of the agricultural population, now, too, more and more superseded by machines.

Engels argued that a permanent improvement can be recognised for two "protected" sections only of the working class, First, the factory hands: "the fixing by Act of Parliament of their working day within relatively rational limits, has restored their physical constitution and endowed them with a moral superiority, enhanced by their local concentration. They are undoubtedly better off than before 1848."

Second, there are unions. "They are the organisations of those trades in which the labour of grown-up men predominates or is alone applicable. Here the competition, neither of women and children nor of machinery, has so far weakened their organised strength. The engineers, the carpenters and joiners, the bricklayers are each of them a power, to that extent that, as in the case of the bricklayers and bricklayers' labourers, they can even successfully resist the introduction of machinery. That their condition has remarkably improved since 1848 there can be no doubt. But as to the great mass of working people, the state of misery and insecurity in which they live now is as low as ever, if not lower."

So at the ripe old age of 24, Engels' close study of the condition of workers in Manchester, England, at the height of the industrial revolution led him to conclude that wage labour was a new form of exploitation from slavery or serfdom peculiar to capitalism. Capitalism through the introduction of technology and machines to replace labour generated a permanent 'reserve army of labour. The size of that reserve army would fluctuate with the vagaries of the industrial cycle of boom and slump under capitalism. But there was always a general downward pressure on workers' wages exerted by capital and thus in the share of income going to labour.

CHAPTER FOUR

Engels on the law of value

Engels on surplus value and labour power

As we saw in Chapter 2, Engels was ahead of Marx in developing a critique of political economy and in an evaluation of the classical law of value as developed by Adam Smith[31] and David Ricardo.[32]. His critique centred on the failure of Ricardo to take into account the anarchy of the market for commodities; and on the other, Jean-Charles Sismondi[33], for ignoring the obvious basis of the value or price of commodities, namely the cost of producing them.

But in his Umrisse, Engels had not developed a theory of value that explained how equal exchange between buyer and seller could lead to profit. That was down to Marx, once he began to study, under the urging of Engels, classical political economy. It was Marx who discovered that capitalist social relations enabled the owners of the means of production to obtain more (as measured in labour time) than they paid the owners of 'labour power', in workers' wages. There was an *equal* exchange in the contract between capitalists and workers, the wage for so many hours. But hidden was the *unequal* exchange of wages for less hours than the value of the commodity produced by the workers and sold by the capitalist on the market. There was surplus value hidden in the 'equal exchange'.

Engels referred to the theory of surplus value as "the pith and marrow" of Marxian political economy and considered that Marx's "two great discoveries", were "the materialistic conception of history and the revelation of the secret of capitalistic production through surplus-value.... With these discoveries socialism became a science".[34]

In his major work, Anti-Duhring written in 1873[35], Engels outlined the importance of Marx's discovery of surplus value: "Marx also discovered the special law of motion governing the present-day capitalist mode of production, and the bourgeois society that this mode of production has created. The discovery of surplus value suddenly threw light on the problem, in trying to solve which all previous investigations, of both bourgeois economists and socialist critics, had been groping in the dark."

Total value in labour time produced by Living Labour

<table>
<tr><td colspan="2" style="text-align:center">The working day</td></tr>
<tr><td>Paid labour =
value of labour power =
wages</td><td>Unpaid labour =
surplus value =
profits, interest, rent</td></tr>
</table>

x labour force (3 bn) =
total hours of labour divided into value of
labour power and surplus value

Engels continues: "Whence comes this surplus-value? It cannot come either from the buyer buying the commodities under their value, or from the seller selling them above their value. For in both cases the gains and the losses of each individual cancel each other, as each individual is in turn buyer and seller. Nor can it come from cheating, for though cheating can enrich one person at the expense of another, it cannot increase the total sum possessed by both, and therefore cannot augment the sum of the values in circulation."

"And yet we find that in each country the capitalist class is continuously enriching itself before our eyes, by selling dearer than it had bought, by appropriating to itself, surplus-value. We are therefore just where we were at the start: whence comes this surplus-value? This problem must be solved, and it must be solved in a *purely economic* way, excluding all cheating and the intervention of any force—the problem being: how is it possible constantly to sell dearer than one has bought, even on the hypothesis that equal values are always exchanged for equal values?"

This solution is as follows: "the increase in the value of money that is to be converted into capital cannot take place in the *money* itself, nor can it originate in the *purchase*, as here this money does no more than realise the price of the commodity, and this price, inasmuch as we took as our premise an exchange of equivalents, is not different from its value. For the same reason, the increase in value cannot originate in the *sale* of the commodity. The change must, therefore, take place in the *commodity* bought; not however in its *value*, as it is bought and sold at its value".

"In order to be able to extract value from the consumption of a commodity, our friend, Moneybags, must be so lucky as to find ... in the market, a commodity, whose use-value possesses the peculiar property of being a source of value, whose actual consumption, therefore, is itself an embodiment of labour, and, consequently, a *creation of value.* The possessor of money does find on the market such a special commodity in capacity for labour or *labour-power."*

This acquires a value from the moment that it becomes a *commodity*, as it is in fact at the present time, and this value is determined, "as in the case of every other commodity, by the labour-time necessary for the production, and consequently also the reproduction, of this special article"; that is to say, by the labour-time necessary for the production of the means of subsistence which the labourer requires for his maintenance in a fit state to work and for the perpetuation of his race.

Let us develop Engels' argument. Let us assume that these means of subsistence represent six hours of labour-time daily. Our capitalist needs to buy some labour-power for carrying out his business. So he hires a labourer and pays this labourer a day's pay for say 12 hours work.. But say this wage as a sum of money represents just six hours of labour, because only six hours' labour is necessary to keep the labourer alive and ready for work. Nothing prevents the capitalist from making the labourer work longer than six hours for a day's pay.

The value of the labour-power, and the value which that labour-power creates in the labour-process, are two different magnitudes. The capitalist owner has paid the value of a day's labour-power in wages but gets the use of that labour power for a day — a whole day's labour (say, 12 hours). Thus, the value of labour created is double the labourer's own value for a day. It's still a fair day's pay for a fair day's work. But the labourer each day *costs* the owner of money the value of the product of six hours' labour, but he *hands over* to the capitalist the value of the product of twelve hours' labour. The capitalist appropriates surplus-value embodied in the product created for which he does not pay. A trick has been performed. Surplus-value has been produced; money has been converted into capital.[36]

In showing how surplus-value arises, and how alone surplus-value can arise under the laws regulating the exchange of commodities, Marx exposed the mechanism of the existing capitalist mode of production and of the mode of appropriation it is based on; he revealed the core around which the whole existing social order has crystallised.

Marx's law of value, his labour theory of value is the litmus test for Marxian political economy. If you do not accept the law as explained by Marx and by Engels (as above), then you cannot be a 'Marxist' economist. Capital does not create value; it only appropriates value from exploiting labour. Only labour creates value.

To talk of 'the productivity of capital' as many, even Marxist economists, do is to confuse this. Engels argues this strongly in his brilliant analysis of fault-lines of the ideas of Pierre Proudhon, the leading socialist radical of Engels' time. Engels disputes the term 'productivity of capital' that Proudhon uses and indeed has become a common term among some Marxists. The "productivity of capital" is an absurdity that Proudhonism takes over uncritically from the bourgeois economists. "The bourgeois economists, it is true, also begin with the statement that labour is the source of all wealth and the measure of value of all commodities; but they also have to explain how it comes about that the capitalist who advances capital for an industrial or handicraft business receives back at the end of it not only the capital which he advanced, but also a profit over and above it. In consequence they are compelled to entangle themselves in all sorts of contradictions and also to ascribe to capital a certain 'pro-ductivity'…. Nothing proves more clearly how deeply Proudhon remains entangled in the bourgeois ideology than the fact that he has taken over this phrase about the productivity of capital. We have already seen at the beginning that the so-called "productivity of capital" is nothing but the quality attached to it (under present-day social relations, without which it would not be capital at all) of being able to appropriate the unpaid labour of wage workers."

Engels was also aware of the alternative to the labour theory of value being promoted by mainstream economics, determined to dismiss the view of the classical economists of early industrial capitalism. "The fashionable theory just now here is that of Stanley Jevons according to which value is determined by utility, i.e. Tauschwert-Gebrauchswert and on the other hand by the limit of supply (i.e. the cost of production), which is merely a confused and circuitous way of saying that value is determined by supply and demand. Vulgar Economy everywhere!"

He was concerned that the socialist movement was also swallowing utility theory. In his Preface to Volume III of Capital, Engels remarked that "George Bernard Shaw was building "the Fabian Church of the Future" on "the foundation of Jevons's and Menger's theory of use-value and marginal utility". Indeed, the Fabians saw themselves, quite consciously, as building a socialism not just different from Marxism but in opposition to it: "there are at the present moment four people in London, calling themselves 'Socialists', who claim to have refuted our author [i.e. Marx] completely by opposing to his theory that of Stanley Jevons!"[37] The utility theory of value, although found faulty by even its own exponents, remains the theory of mainstream economics today – an example of the bankruptcy of economic theory.[38]

Engels on value and money
Engels' particular contribution to Marx's law of value and surplus value was to explain its historical development. This is developed in Anti-Duhring. Engels argues that the relation between the owners of money or of commodities on the one hand, and those who possess nothing beyond their own labour-power on the other, is not a natural relation, nor is it one that is common to all historical periods: "It is clearly the result of a past historical development, the product ... of the extinction of a whole series of older forms of social production."

Surplus-labour, labour beyond the time required for the labourer's own maintenance, and appropriation by others of the product of this surplus-labour, the exploitation of labour, is common to all forms of society that have existed hitherto. But it is only when the product of this surplus-labour assumes the form of surplus-value, when the owner of the means of production finds the free labourer—free from social fetters and free from possessions of his own—as an object of exploitation, and exploits him for the purpose of the production of commodities for sale—it is only then that the means of production assume the specific character of capital.

Engels proposes that this first took place on a large scale at the end of the 15th and the beginning of the 16th century as a result of the dissolution of the feudal mode of production. With this, however, and with the bringing into being of world trade and the world market dating from the same epoch, the basis was established on which the mass of the existing movable wealth was necessarily more and more converted into capital, and the capitalist mode of production, aimed at the creation of surplus-value, necessarily became more and more exclusively the prevailing mode.

Engels then raises the question of the emergence of money. There was money before capitalism, but only under the capitalist mode of production, does money become capital, ie where money is used to buy labour power to exploit for surplus value. Once commodity production for surplus value becomes the dominant mode, so money emerges universally and can be transformed into capital. "As a matter of history, capital, as opposed to landed property, invariably takes the form at first of money; it appears as moneyed wealth, as the capital of the merchant and of the usurer... We can see it daily under our very eyes. All new capital, to commence with, comes on the stage, that is, on the market, whether of commodities, labour, or money, even in our days, in the shape of money that by a definite process has to be transformed into capital."

The next stage in the "subjugation of industry by capital" entails the transition to manufacturing. Here "the surplus value appropriated by the manufacturing capitalist enables him (or the export merchant who shares with him) to sell cheaper than his competitors" – handicraftsmen – "until the general introduction of the new mode of production, when equalization again takes place.

It is large-scale industry that thus finally conquers the domestic market for capital, puts an end to the small-scale production and natural economy of the self-sufficient peasant family, eliminates direct exchange between small producers and places the entire nation in the service of capital. Likewise, it equalises the profit rate of the different commercial and industrial branches of business into *one* general rate of profit, and finally ensures industry the position of power due to it in this equalisation by eliminating most of the obstacles formerly hindering the transfer of capital from one branch to another. Thus, for Engels, the law of value is historically determined and exists in prevailing form only in modern capitalism.

Looking back at his critique of classical political economy in the 1870s, Engels commented: "Political economy is therefore essentially a historical science. It deals with material which is historical, that is, constantly changing; it must first investigate the special laws of each individual stage in the evolution of production and exchange, and only when it has completed this investigation will it be able to establish the few quite general laws which hold good for production and exchange in general."

He goes on: "the conditions under which men produce and exchange vary from country to country, and within each country again from generation to generation. Political economy, therefore, cannot be the same for all countries and for all historical epochs. A tremendous distance separates the bow and arrow, the stone knife and the acts of exchange among savages occurring only by way of exception, from the steam-engine of a thousand horse power, the mechanical loom, the railways and the Bank of England. The inhabitants of Tierra del Fuego have not got so far as mass production and world trade, any more than they have experience of bill-jobbing or a Stock Exchange crash. Anyone who attempted to bring the political economy of Tierra del Fuego under the same laws as are operative in present-day England would obviously produce nothing but the most banal commonplaces."

Engels' view has come under attack since by Marxists. He has been accused of arguing that the law of value has always existed in class societies and would even continue under socialism. But this is not Engels' view. In Anti-Duhring, he is clear that surplus value would not exist in a communist (socialist) society where the production of use values and their distribution is achieved through common ownership, democratic decision and by direct consumption, not by the exploitation of labour power by capital or through market competition. "I should delimit [the concept of value] historically by expressly confining [it] to the economic phase in which alone there has and could have been any question of value hitherto – to the social forms in which exchange of commodities and production of commodities exist; primitive communism was innocent of value." (Engels).

Engels on the transformation of values into prices

Engels showed how Marx took value theory beyond classical political economy. "By substituting labour power, the value-producing property, for labour [Marx] solved with one stroke one of the difficulties which brought about the downfall of the Ricardian school, viz., the impossibility of harmonizing the mutual exchange of capital and labour with the Ricardian law that value is determined by labour." That labour paid a competitive wage determined by "mutual exchange" but nonetheless generated a surplus was one of two "difficulties" relating to surplus value – the second involved the transformation issue – that had brought about the "shipwreck" of the Ricardian school in 1830 or thereabouts.

Engels adds to Marx's explanation of how market prices are connected to commodity values measured in labour time – the so-called transformation issue. Apart from explaining Marx's transformation solution, he emphasises the historical development of this transformation. Some have argued that this would not have been acceptable to Marx. Again, this is wrong. As Marx said himself: "it is quite appropriate to regard the values of commodities as not only theoretically but also historically *prius* to the prices of production."

In defending Marx's theory, Engels spent much ink in showing how rival theories of surplus were not up to the task compared to that of Marx. His main focus was on Johann Rodbertus, a German economist and socialist.[39], who claimed that he had discovered 'surplus value' before Marx. Engels retorted that "Rodbertus adopts the traditional definitions of economic concepts entirely in the form in which they have come down to him from the economists. He does not make the slightest attempt to investigate them. Value is for him 'the valuation of one thing against others according to quantity, this valuation being conceived as measure'. Marx's surplus value, on the contrary, represents the *general form* of the sum of values appropriated without any equivalent by the owners of the means of production, and this form splits into the distinct, *converted* forms of profit and ground rent in accordance with very specific laws, which Marx was the first to discover." He explained that there were "many intermediate links . . . required to arrive from an understanding of surplus value in general at an understanding of its transformation into profit and ground rent; in other words, at an understanding of the laws of the distribution of surplus value within the capitalist class".

Unlike Rodbertus, Engels points out that Marx's theory of surplus value puts rent, profit and interest as *parts* of surplus value, not independent sources of income outside the creation of value by labour power. This was the error of Adam Smith's value theory, which Rodbertus had adopted. The making of rent or profit or interest as separate sources of value is still happening in modern heterodox economics and among those claiming to have a Marxian value theory.[40]

Engels, in his Preface to Marx's Capital Volume 2, which he had edited, challenged readers to show how an equal average rate of profit can and must come about not only without a violation of the law of value, but rather on the very basis of it.. Several had a go. Achille Loria[41] reckoned that it was impossible to reconcile the labour theory of value with market prices. He reckoned that Marx's transformation solution was really an abandonment of the labour theory, because it meant using prices of production and doing away with labour values. Loria's objection preceded many such revisionist theories from modern mainstream economist Paul Samuelson[42] to the theory of 'commodities by commodities' of 'Keynesian/Marxist' Piero Sraffa.[43] Samuelson put it thus: "Marx set out with an erroneous value scheme, erased it, and started anew with a true price scheme" (Samuelson 1971: 421).

But a third contributor, writing in *Conrad's Jahrbucher* in 1892, "placed his finger on the salient point" (Engels). Peter Fireman[44] explained how surplus value, depending on the exploitation of labour – unpaid labour – and so proportional to the labour input, gets transferred into a uniform return on capital through market competition. Fireman: "Simply by selling commodities above their value in all branches of production in which the ratio between . . . constant and variable capital is greatest; but this also implies that commodities are sold below their value in those branches of production in which the ratio between constant and variable capital = c:v is smallest, and that commodities are sold at their true value only in branches in which the ratio of c:v represents a certain mean figure.". Fireman concludes "Is this discrepancy between individual prices and their respective values a refutation of the value principle? By no means. For since the prices of some commodities rise above their value as much as the prices of others fall below it, the total sum of prices remains equal to the total sum of values . . . in the end this incongruity disappears."

In a letter to German economist Werner Sombart[45], Engels argued that "[t]he conceptual transitions whereby Marx arrives at the general and equal rate of profit from the various values produced in individual capitalist concerns . . . are wholly foreign to the consciousness of the individual capitalist" (MECW *50*: 460). Each individual capitalist merely seeks to maximize his profits, and "[b]ourgeois economics reveals that this pursuit of *bigger* profits on the part of each individual capitalist results in a general and *equal* rate of profit, an approximately equal rate of profit for all. But neither capitalists nor bourgeois economists are aware that the real purpose of that pursuit is the equal percentual distribution of the total surplus value over capital as a whole".

Engels rejected the charge that the transformation of values into prices of production through competition was some sort of "theoretically necessary fiction." For Engels, that was quite incorrect. The law of value has a far greater and more definite significance for capitalist production than of a mere hypothesis, not to mention a fiction, even though a necessary one. "We are dealing here not only with a purely logical process but with a real historical process."

Engels points out that all theoretical models in economics (and in the sciences) are approximations. If, for example, "we were to insist that the rate of profit – say, 14.876934 . . . be exactly the same down to the last decimal point in every business every year, on pain of being reduced to a fiction, we should be grossly mistaking the nature of the rate of profit and of economic laws generally – none of them have any reality save as an approximation, a tendency, an average, but not an immediate reality. This is due partly to the fact that their action is frustrated by the simultaneous action of other laws, but also to some extent by their nature as concepts." So "total profit and the total surplus value can correspond only approximately," a tendency only, the "unity of concept and phenomenon . . . an essentially endless process"

Engels hits the nail on the head here. Scientific method is aimed at finding the truth about phenomena and above all trying to develop laws that can explain cause and effect. If we leave analysis to just description: namely that this happened and then this happened etc, we explain nothing. Marx's dialectical method was first to start with the surface events and then drill down to the underlying abstraction or essence of the process, namely the underlying laws of motion of capitalism. Then once that had been identified, namely the nature of the commodity and the law of value, the scientist can work back to the level of appearance and thus dialectically reveal the causes of everyday events.

The best economic theory and explanation comes from looking at the aggregate, the average and its outliers. Data based on a few studies or data points provide no explanatory power. A scientific approach would aim to test theory against the evidence on a continual basis, not just to falsify it (as the liberal Karl Popper[46] would have it) but also to strengthen its explanatory power – unless a better explanation of the facts comes along. Newton's theory of gravity explained very much about the universe and was tested by the evidence, but then Einstein's theory of relativity came along and better explained the facts (or widened our understanding to things that could not be explained by Newton's laws). In this sense, the Marxist method is also scientific. Marx went from the abstract (theory) to the concrete (facts). The facts would then strengthen the explanatory power of the theory or modify it.

Engels on 'secondary exploitation'

The nature of the relationship between profit, rent and interest was taken up by Engels in his ground-breaking pamphlet on housing.[47] In the Holy Family written jointly with Marx in 1845, but mainly by Engels, Engels criticises the leading socialist of the time, Pierre-Joseph Proudhon for wanting to maintain the capitalist social relations of wages, prices and money in any future socialist society as they are "forms of private property in themselves." [48] Proudhon's policy proposal to deal with the lack of decent housing at reasonable cost to working people was for cooperative "self-help" measures by labour – pre-eminently building societies that act as a sort of savings bank. In the Holy Family, Engels rejected this as building cooperatives were not essentially workers' societies; as their chief aim was to provide "a more profitable mortgage investment for the savings of the petty bourgeoisie, at a good rate of interest," with a "prospect of dividends from speculation in real estate".

During the 1870s, a major polemical debate unfolded in Germany's worker/democratic press on the shortage of housing available to workers in major industrial centres. The influx and increase of the proletariat created a housing crisis. In 1872, Engels contributed the first of a series of articles to the *Volksstaat*, entitled "The Housing Question."

Engels' central point was that the housing question could not be resolved within the confines of the market because "it is not that the solution of the housing question simultaneously solves the social question, but that only by the solution of the social question, that is, by the abolition of the capitalist mode of production, is the solution of the housing question made possible."

Engels argued that if high rents (or in modern terms, costly mortgage costs) became the norm, then workers would have to build that into their minimum requirement for living as the value of labour power was socially determined, not just physically. So a solution to the "housing question" based on worker ownership of their homes could, at best, only be temporary and would reduce cooperation among workers and have the effect of turning the clock back in favour of pre capitalist domestic industry. Home ownership acts as a fetter on the ability of working people to move where they wish: "the housing shortage is no accident; it is a necessary institution and can be abolished together with all its effects on health, etc., only if the whole social order from which it springs is fundamentally refashioned."

Engels took deadly aim at the arguments of two giants in this debate, Proudhon and also Austrian economist Emil Sax[49]. Proudhon proposed an end to private landlordism via the conversion of tenants' rents into purchase payments on their dwellings, which he believed would end exploitative relations between landlords and tenants that had led to so much suffering at the time. Social reformer Sax held the view that 'home-and-garden' ownership would transform workers into capitalists by enabling them to generate income or credit from real estate in hard times and also improve their sense of self-worth.

In contrast, Engels, believed that homeownership would in fact "chain the worker in semi-feudal fashion to his own particular capitalist". For Engels, private property rights were far from liberating for workers; they constituted the chief institutional arrangement that made capitalist urban expansion possible, encompassing all the myriad features of political economy (wages, trade, value, price, money) that he had seen at work in Manchester, and that were responsible for the creation of stark inequalities, grotesque exploitation, and appalling injustices. Far from embracing private property rights, Engels continued, any revolutionary movement had to acknowledge their central role in creating a society thoroughly driven and moulded by the interests of capital accumulation at the expense of working people.

For Engels there was no such thing as a housing crisis[50], only a crisis of capitalism in which housing conditions formed just 'one of the innumerable, smaller, secondary evils' caused by the exploitation of workers by capital. ... From this flowed two inescapable conclusions: the first was that workers, not tenants, were the agents of change in capitalist society; and, secondly, the only real alternative to the housing question was 'to abolish altogether the exploitation and oppression of the working class by the ruling class' through working class revolution and the expropriation of private property.

Engels' critique has modern relevance. Take Margaret Thatcher's highly popular move in the UK in the 1980s to encourage direct sales of council housing at very large discounts to tenants – to expand homeownership at the expense of the public housing stock. This Right to Buy policy is now the one direct and major cause of the lack of affordable housing in the UK today (over the past 35 years, nearly 3 million publicly owned homes have been sold off under the scheme).

The Right to Buy even failed on its own privatising terms, as many who exercised their Right to Buy sold on to private landlords, who rented them to tenants at double or triple the levels of private rent, which required tenants to apply for housing benefit from the state. So Thatcher's flagship policy actually ended up costing the state far more in housing benefit than it ever did in maintenance and management of council homes.

As Engels put it: "The cornerstone of the capitalist mode of production is, however, the fact that our present social order enables the capitalists to buy the labour power of the worker at its value, but to extract from it much more than its value by making the worker work longer than is necessary in order to reproduce the price paid for the labour power. The surplus value produced in this fashion is divided among the whole class of capitalists and landowners together with their paid servants, from the Pope and the Kaiser, down to the night watchman and below. We are not concerned here as to how this distribution comes about, but this much is certain: that all those who do not work can live only from fragments of this surplus value which reach them in one way or another."

Engels goes on to make a very important distinction between exploitation of the worker in capitalist production for surplus value appropriated by the capitalist and swindling of workers and other classes by landlords with high rents and bankers with high interest rates on loans. "The distribution of this surplus value, produced by the working class and taken from it without payment, among the non-working classes proceeds amid extremely edifying squabblings and mutual swindling. In so far as this distribution takes place by means of buying and selling, one of its chief methods is the cheating of the buyer by the seller, and in retail trade, particularly in the big towns, this has become an absolute condition of existence for the sellers."

Swindling is the norm , but "when, however, the worker is cheated by his grocer or his baker, either in regard to the price or the quality of the commodity, this does not happen to him in his specific capacity as a worker. On the contrary, as soon as a certain average level of cheating has become the social rule in any place, it must in the long run be levelled out by a corresponding increase in wages. The worker appears before the small shopkeeper as a buyer, that is, as the owner of money or credit, and hence not at all in his capacity as a worker, that is, as a seller of labour power. The cheating may hit him, and the poorer class as a whole, harder than it hits the richer social classes, but it is not an evil which hits him exclusively or is peculiar to his class."

The growth of the big modern cities gives the land in certain areas, particularly in those which are centrally situated, an artificial and often colossally increasing value. So the buildings erected on these areas are not nearly decisive in the cost of housing. They can be pulled down and replaced by others. This takes place above all with workers' houses which are situated centrally. It's the land that matters for the developer. Workers' housing at cheap rents can be pulled down and in their stead shops, warehouses and public buildings are erected at higher rents.

Engels recalls that through the Haussmann construction program in Paris after the defeat of the 1848 revolutions, Louis Bonaparte exploited this tendency tremendously for swindling and private enrichment. "The spirit of Haussmann has also been abroad in London, Manchester and Liverpool, and seems to feel itself just as much at home in Berlin and Vienna. The result is that the workers are forced out of the centre of the towns towards the outskirts; that workers' dwellings, and small dwellings in general, become rare and expensive and often altogether unobtainable, for under these circumstances the building industry, which is offered a much better field for speculation by more expensive houses, builds workers' dwellings only by way of exception." When we look at the state of the housing market today in the major advanced capitalist economies, we can see that nothing much has changed from Engels' analysis in 1879. 'Affordable housing, let alone social housing, has diminished dramatically since the days of public housing programmes.

Proudhon's view at the time was "as the wage worker in relation to the capitalist, so is the tenant in relation to the house owner."[51] The idea that exploitation at the workplace is repeated in workers' consumption of housing needs has been adopted by some modern Marxists like David Harvey or Costas Lapavitsas and this exploitative relationship is just as important, if not more so, as a hotspot for class struggle ie between tenant and landlord or mortgage lender as between workers and capitalist.[52]

Engels on the housing question

In his Housing Question, Engels begs to disagree with the Proudhonist view. In the housing question we have two parties confronting each other: the tenant and the landlord or house owner. The former wishes to purchase from the latter the temporary use of a dwelling; he has money or credit, even if he has to buy this credit from the house owner himself at a usurious price as an addition to the rent. It is simple commodity sale; it is not an operation between proletarian and bourgeois, between worker and capitalist. The tenant – even if he is a worker – appears as a man with money; he must already have sold his own particular commodity, his labour power, in order to appear with the proceeds as the buyer of the use of a dwelling, or he must be in a position to give a guarantee of the impending sale of this labour power"

The peculiar results which attend the sale of labour power to the capitalist are completely absent here. The capitalist causes the purchased labour power firstly to produce its own value and secondly to produce a surplus value which remains in his hands for the time being, subject to its distribution among the capitalist class. In this case therefore an extra value is produced, the total sum of the existing value is increased. In the rent transaction the situation is quite different. No matter how much the landlord may overreach the tenant it is still only a transfer of already existing, previously produced value, and the total sum of values possessed by the landlord and the tenant together remains the same after as it was before.

The worker is always cheated of a part of the product of his labour, whether that labour is paid for by the capitalist below, above, or at its value. The tenant, on the other hand, is cheated only when he is compelled to pay for the dwelling above its value. It is, therefore, a complete misrepresentation of the relation between landlord and tenant to attempt to make it equivalent to the relation between worker and capitalist. On the contrary, we are dealing here with a quite ordinary commodity transaction between two citizens, and this transaction proceeds according to the economic laws which govern the sale of commodities in general and in particular the sale of the commodity, land property. The building and maintenance costs of the house, or of the part of the house in question, enters first of all into the calculation; the land value, determined by the more or less favourable situation of the house, comes next; the state of the relation between supply and demand existing at the moment is finally decisive."

Nothing could be clearer here that Engels does not consider the land-lord/tenant relationship or the banker/householder relationship as exploitation in the capitalist sense. Trying to get a fair transaction for housing through rent to a landlord or a mortgage from a bank does not change the structure of the exploitation process under capitalism. "The petty-bourgeois Proudhon demands a world in which each person turns out a separate and independent product that is immediately consumable and exchangeable in the market. Then, as long as each person only receives back the full value of his labour in the form of another product, "eternal justice" is satisfied and the best possible world created. The capitalist mode of production, the basis of present-day society, is in no way affected. The pivot on which the exploitation of the worker turns is the sale of labour power to the capitalist and the use which the capitalist makes of this transaction in that he compels the worker to produce far more than the paid value of the labour power amounts to. It is this transaction between capitalist and worker which produces all the surplus value which is afterwards divided in the form of ground rent, commercial profit, interest on capital, taxes, etc., among the various sub-species of capitalists and their servants."

That makes any policy aimed at controlling or stopping landlords from getting rents or bankers interest as falling well short of solving the 'housing question'. "And now our Proudhonist comes along and believes that if we were to forbid one single sub-species of capitalists, and at that of such capitalists who purchase no labour power directly and therefore also cause no surplus value to be produced, to receive profit or interest, it would be a step forward! The mass of unpaid labour taken from the working class would remain exactly the same even if house owners were to be deprived tomorrow of the possibility of receiving ground rent and interest."

In this way, Engels rejects the argument of some modern Marxists that it is finance capital that is now the enemy of the working class because of the interest charged on loans. "The interest on loaned money capital is only a part of profit; profit, whether on industrial or commercial capital, is only a part of the surplus value taken by the capitalist class from the working class in the form of unpaid labour.

The rate of interest does not affect the rate of surplus value extracted by the capitalist. "The economic laws which govern the rate of interest are as independent of those which govern the rate of surplus value as could possibly be the case between laws of one and the same social form". Thus "The reduction and final abolition of interest would therefore by no means really take the so-called "productivity of capital" "by the horns"; it would do no more than re-arrange the distribution among the individual capitalists of the unpaid surplus value taken from the working class; it would not, therefore, give an advantage to the worker as against the industrial capitalist, but to the industrial capitalist as against the rentier…The mass of surplus value extracted from the working class by the capitalist class would remain the same; only its distribution would be altered, and even that not much."

Presaging the modern mainstream argument that debt matters and must be repaid, whether state or private debt, Engels states: "for the bourgeois, and in particular for the petty bourgeois, credit is an important matter and it would therefore be a very fine thing for them, and in particular for the petty bourgeois, if credit could be obtained at any time and, in addition, without payment of interest. A very high proportion of workers pay rent and do not have mortgages; so the cost of credit for housing is not a significant issue: "private debt or credit interest the bourgeoisie very much, but the worker only very little. …All these things which are held up to us here as highly important questions for the working class are in reality of essential interest only to the bourgeoisie, and in particular to the petty bourgeoisie, and, despite Proudhon, we assert that the working class is not called upon to look after the interests of these classes."

Today, against environmental managerialism, an 'Engelsian' approach would focus on features of urban design, housing provision and construction, land tenure, access to clean water and fresh air, and safe and healthy working relations and conditions in their relationship to the human, social and developmental needs of individuals and families.

Engels's analysis was based on his firm and carefully evidenced association of the environmental costs of industrialization with social class.

Residential segregation and urban design in general enabled the beneficiaries of the new industrial capitalist order to shield themselves both from the direct environmental destruction it left in its wake, and from the disturbing sight of the human price paid by others for their affluence. For Engels, there were clear, if complex, causal connections between industrial wage labour, hazard at work, poor and adulterated diet, inadequate clothing, air and water pollution, overcrowded, damp and unhygienic housing, anxiety, demoralization, sickness and early death.

Engels on nature and value

Marx and Engels are often accused of what has been called a Promethean[53] vision of human social organisation, namely that human beings, using knowledge and technical prowess, can and should impose their will on the rest of the planet and what is called 'nature' – for better or worse.

The charge is that other living species are merely playthings for the use of human beings. There are humans and there is nature - in contradiction. This charge is particularly aimed at Engels, who it is claimed took a bourgeois 'positivist' view of science: scientific knowledge was progressive and neutral in ideology; and so was the relationship between man and nature. Indeed, the modern 'green' critique of Marx and Engels is that they were unaware that homo sapiens were destroying the planet and thus themselves. Instead Marx and Engels had a touching Promethean faith in capitalism's ability to develop the productive forces and technology to overcome any risks to the planet and nature.

That Marx and Engels paid no attention to the impact on nature of human social activity has been debunked recently in particular by the ground-breaking work of Marxist authors like John Bellamy Foster and Paul Burkett[54]. They have reminded us throughout Marx's Capital, Marx was very aware of capitalism's degrading impact on nature and the resources of the planet. Marx wrote that "the capitalist mode of production collects the population together in great centres and causes the urban population to achieve an ever-growing preponderance…. [It] disturbs the metabolic interaction between man and the earth, i.e., it prevents the return to the soil of its constituent elements consumed by man in the form of food and clothing; hence it hinders the operation of the eternal natural condition for the lasting fertility of the soil. Thus, it destroys at the same time the physical health of the urban worker, and the intellectual life of the rural worker."

As Paul Burkett says: "it is difficult to argue that there is something fundamentally anti-ecological about Marx's analysis of capitalism and his projections of communism." To back this up, Kohei Saito's recent book has drawn on Marx's previously unpublished 'excerpt' notebooks in the ongoing MEGA research project to reveal Marx's extensive study of scientific works of the time on agricultures, soil, forestry to expand his concept of the connection between capitalism and its destruction of natural resources.[55]

But Engels too must be saved from the same charge. Engels was well ahead of Marx (yet again) in connecting the destruction and damage to the environment that industrialisation was causing. While still living in his home town of Barmen (now Wuppertal), he wrote several diary notes about the inequality of rich and poor, the pious hypocrisy of the church preachers and also the pollution of the rivers. Just 18 years old, he writes: "the two towns of Elberfeld and Barmen, which stretch along the valley for a distance of nearly three hours' travel. The purple waves of the narrow river flow sometimes swiftly, sometimes sluggishly between smoky factory buildings and yarn-strewn bleaching-yards. Its bright red colour, however, is due not to some bloody battle, for the fighting here is waged only by theological pens and garrulous old women, usually over trifles, nor to shame for men's actions, although there is indeed enough cause for that, but simply and solely to the numerous dye-works using Turkey red. Coming from Düsseldorf, one enters the sacred region at Sonnborn; the muddy Wupper flows slowly by and, compared with the Rhine just left behind, its miserable appearance is very disappointing."

He goes on: "First and foremost, factory work is largely responsible. Work in low rooms where people breathe more coal fumes and dust than oxygen — and in the majority of cases beginning already at the age of six — is bound to deprive them of all strength and joy in life."

He connected the social degradation of working families with the degradation of nature alongside the hypocritical piety of the manufacturers. "Terrible poverty prevails among the lower classes, particularly the

Barmen in 1913

factory workers in Wuppertal; syphilis and lung diseases are so widespread as to be barely credible; in Elberfeld alone, out of 2,500 children of school age 1,200 are deprived of education and grow up in the factories — merely so that the manufacturer need not pay the adults, whose place they take, twice the wage he pays a child. But the wealthy manufacturers have a flexible conscience and causing the death of one child more or one less does not doom a pietist's soul to hell, especially if he goes to church twice every Sunday. For it is a fact that the pietists among the factory owners treat their workers worst of all; they use every possible means to reduce the workers' wages on the pretext of depriving them of the opportunity to get drunk, yet at the election of preachers they are always the first to bribe their people."[56]

Sure, these observations by Engels were just that, observations, without any theoretical development, but they show the sensitivity that Engels already had to the relationship between industrialisation, the owners and the workers, their poverty and the environmental impact of factory production.

In Umrisse, Engels noted how the private ownership of the land, the drive for profit and the degradation of nature go hand in hand. "To make earth an object of huckstering — the earth which is our one and all, the first condition of our existence — was the last step towards making oneself an object of huckstering. It was and is to this very day an immorality surpassed only by the immorality of self-alienation. And the original appropriation — the monopolization of the earth by a few, the exclusion of the rest from that which is the condition of their life — yields nothing in immorality to the subsequent huckstering of the earth." Once the earth becomes commodified by capital, it is subject to just as much degradation as labour.

Engels' major work (with Marx's help), The Dialectics of Nature, published in 1883 just after Marx's death, is often subject to attack as extending Marx's materialist conception of history as applied to humans, into nature in a non-Marxist way. And yet, in his book, Engels could not be clearer on the dialectical relation between humans and nature.[57]

In a famous chapter "The Role of Work in Transforming Ape into Man.", he writes:

"Let us not, however, flatter ourselves overmuch on account of our human conquest over nature. For each such conquest takes its revenge on us. Each of them, it is true, has in the first place the consequences on which we counted, but in the second and third places it has quite different, unforeseen effects which only too often cancel out the first. The people who, in Mesopotamia, Greece, Asia Minor, and elsewhere, destroyed the forests to obtain cultivable land, never dreamed that they were laying the basis for the present devastated condition of these countries, by removing along with the forests the collecting centres and reservoirs of moisture. When, on the southern slopes of the mountains, the Italians of the Alps used up the pine forests so carefully cherished on the northern slopes, they had no inkling that by doing so they were … thereby depriving their mountain springs of water for the greater part of the year, with the effect that these would be able to pour still more furious flood torrents on the plains during the rainy seasons. Those who spread the potato in Europe were not aware that they were at the same time spreading the disease of scrofula. Thus at every step we are reminded that we by no means rule over nature like a conqueror over a foreign people, like someone standing outside nature — but that we, with flesh, blood, and brain, belong to nature, and exist in its midst, and that all our mastery of it consists in the fact that we have the advantage over all other beings of being able to know and correctly apply its laws."

Engels goes on: "in fact, with every day that passes we are learning to understand these laws more correctly and getting to know both the more immediate and the more remote consequences of our interference with the traditional course of nature. … But the more this happens, the more

Slave market in the New World

Sugar plantation in the Caribbean

will men not only feel, but also know, their unity with nature, and thus the more impossible will become the senseless and antinatural idea of a contradiction between mind and matter, man and nature, soul and body. …"

Engels explains the social consequences of the drive to expand the productive forces. "But if it has already required the labour of thousands of years for us to learn to some extent to calculate the more remote natural consequences of our actions aiming at production, it has been still more difficult in regard to the more remote social consequences of these actions. … When afterwards Columbus discovered America, he did not know that by doing so he was giving new life to slavery, which in Europe had long ago been done away with; and laying the basis for the Negro slave traffic. …"

The people of the Americas were driven into slavery, but also nature was enslaved. As Engels put it: "What cared the Spanish planters in Cuba, who burned down forests on the slopes of the mountains and obtained from the ashes sufficient fertilizer for one generation of very highly profitable

The plague

coffee trees–what cared they that the heavy tropical rainfall afterwards washed away the unprotected upper stratum of the soil, leaving behind only bare rock!" .

Now we know that it was not just slavery that the Europeans brought to the Americas, but also disease, which in its many forms exterminated 90% of native Americans and was the main reason for their subjugation by colonialism. [58]

After the experience of COVID-19 in the 21st century, we now know that it was capitalism's drive to industrialise agriculture and usurp the remaining wilderness that has led to nature 'striking back', as humans come into contact with pathogens to which they have no immunity, just as the native Americans in the 16th century.[59]

In pre-capitalist societies where there was common ownership, the ravaging of the land was avoided. In an appendix to his 1892 pamphlet, Socialism Utopian and Scientific, Engels gives an account of commons-based communities in parts of pre-capitalist Germany: "[T]he use of arable and meadowlands was under the supervision and direction of the community …"Just as the share of each member in so much of the mark as was distributed was of equal size, so was his share also in the use of the 'common mark.' The nature of this use was determined by the members of the community as a whole. … "At fixed times and, if necessary, more frequently, they met in the open air to discuss the affairs of the mark and to sit in judgment upon breaches of regulations and disputes concerning the mark." [60]

Historians and other scholars have broadly confirmed Engels' description of communal management of shared resources. A summary of recent research concluded: "[W]hat existed in fact was not a 'tragedy of the commons' but rather a triumph: that for hundreds of years — and perhaps thousands, although written records do not exist to prove the longer era — land was managed successfully by communities."[61]

The need for common ownership and the managing of nature for all is particularly necessary with agriculture. As Marx argued in Capital Volume 3: "nature requires long cycles of birth, development and regeneration, but capitalism requires short-term returns. [T]he entire spirit of capitalist production, which is oriented towards the most immediate monetary profits, stands in contradiction to agriculture, which has to concern itself with the whole gamut of permanent conditions of life required by the chain of human generations. A striking illustration of this is furnished by the forests, which are only rarely managed in a way more or less corresponding to the interests of society as a whole…"[62]

A community that shares fields and forests has a strong incentive to protect them to the best of its ability, even if that means not maximizing current production, because those resources will be essential to the community's survival for centuries to come. Capitalist owners have the opposite incentive, because they will not survive in business if they don't maximize short-term profit. If ethanol promises bigger and faster profits than centuries-old rain forests, the trees will fall. [63]

Engels attacked the view that 'human nature' is inherently selfish and will just destroy nature. In his Outline, Engels described that argument as a "repulsive blasphemy against man and nature." Humans can work in harmony with and as part of nature. It requires greater knowledge of the consequences of human action. Engels said in his Dialectics: "But even in this sphere, by long and often cruel experience and by collecting and analyzing the historical material, we are gradually learning to get a clear view of the indirect, more remote, social effects of our productive activity, and so the possibility is afforded us of mastering and controlling these effects as well."

But better knowledge and scientific progress is not enough. For Marx and Engels, the possibility of ending the dialectical contradiction between man and nature and bringing about some level of harmony and ecological balance would only be possible with the abolition of the capitalist mode of production. Climate activist, Greta Thunbergh, recently said that "the climate and ecological crisis cannot be solved within today's political and economic systems. That isn't an opinion. That's a fact." And as Engels said: "To carry out this control requires something more than mere knowledge." Science is not enough. "It requires a complete revolution in our hitherto existing mode of production, and with it of our whole contemporary social order." The 'positivist' Engels, it seems, still supported Marx's materialist conception of history.

Engels made his own contribution to the Marxian law of value apart from explaining clearly Marx's value theory. He attacked the concept of the 'productivity of capital' he showed correctly the historical origins of value and commodity production; he explained and defended Marx's transformation of values into prices of production in the market and he refuted the views that there were other forms of profit creation and other decisive forms of class struggle eg landlord versus tenant; banker versus householder, rather than worker versus capitalist. Most significant for modern times, he showed that capital was not only exploiting labour but also destroying the planet in the process. Nature and humanity should be in harmony, but that is impossible under capitalism.

CHAPTER FIVE

Engels and the law of profitability

Engels defends the law of profitability

Engels was firmly committed to Marx's law of the tendency for the rate of profit to fall, as expounded in Volume 3, as the underlying cause of crises under capitalism. Just as Marx did, Engels saw the law of profitability as a tendency. Engels points out that Marx considered his analysis of "the tendency of the profit rate to fall as society progresses" to be "one of the greatest triumphs over all previous political economy".[64]. Engels too considered that Marx's law of profitability was an essential feature of Marx's analysis. The law depended on Marx's other key laws: the law of value and the law of accumulation, to which Engels was committed, as we have seen in previous chapters. From these laws, the law of the tendency of the rate of profit to fall follows.[65]

Behind commercial and financial crises lay the underlying health of British capitalism – and that ultimately depended on the profitability of industrial capital. From the very beginning, Marxian political economy puts profit and profitability of capital at the centre of the capitalist production process. Obviously, if wages fall, profits will rise. But following Adam Smith, increased competition between capitals will bring the profit rate down once again: "the manufacturers have in view solely the immediate advantage which the repeal of the Corn Laws would bring them. They are too narrow-minded to see that, even for themselves, no permanent advantage can arise from this measure, because their competition with each other would soon force the profit of the individual back to its old level".

This is not Marx's eventual explanation for the tendency of the rate of profit to fall, but back in the 1840s, Engels had only Smith's theory of profitability to rely on namely that an individual capitalist looks to raise his/her profit rate, but no permanent advantage is possible because of competition and eventually any increase subsides.

The rate of profit may fall over the long term, but not in a straight line. There can be periods when profitability rises at the expense of labour. Allen finds that profit rates for British capital rose substantially during the war with Republican France and then stagnated or subsided in the post-war period up to the 1830s. In the 1830s, there was a sharp rise reaching a peak just before Engels arrived in England. The 1840s was a period of downwave in profitability for capital, real wages for workers and successive slumps. After the failure of the Chartist movement and 1848 revolutions, the scene was set for a long boom in profitability and growth until 1870.[66]

Marxian profit-rate theory itself required preliminary comprehension of the surplus-value doctrine. Engels insisted on the downward secular trend as an essential feature of Marx's analysis. In March 1895 he congratulated Conrad Schmidt[67] on his keen appreciation of the phenomenon, more specifically, that the "motive for accumulation will diminish with every diminution of profit".

It is ironic that Marx's most important law in political economy has been neglected, ignored or dismissed, not just by mainstream economics (which is not surprising), but also by so-called heterodox economics and by the bulk of Marxist economists. And yet the law is logical and consistent as theory and is also backed up by an ever-growing quantity of empirical evidence.[68] Engels praised Schmidt because "his is the honour of independently finding the correct explanation developed by Marx in the third part of the third volume for the hitherto inexplicable sinking tendency of the rate of profit."

Engels also maintained that the law had empirical backing, referring to an empirical study of the US profit-rate trend of 1870–80, according to which the profit rate had fallen, rejecting another critic's view, Georg Stiebeling,[69] who "interprets it wrongly and assumes that Marx's theory of a constantly stable rate of profit should be corrected on the basis of experience" – a "stable rate" being a "figment of Mr. Stiebeling's imagination.". To the contrary, Engels comments that Stiebeling "proves, for instance, by comparing US census figures for 1870 and 1880 that the rate of profit has actually fallen."[70] Modern research confirms Engels' conclusion about the rate of profit in 1870s and 1880s.[71]

Engels on the turnover of capital

In Capital Volume 3, Engels adds to Marx's law of profitability his own original analysis of the turnover of capital. Having discussed this with Marx in a series of letters, Engels draws directly upon his own knowledge of cotton manufacturing to develop the importance of the 'moral depreciation' of constant capital, namely the fall in the cost of the means of production through innovation, which can act as a counterfactor to the tendency of the rate of profit to fall. Modern Marxist political economy has generally failed to understand Engels' important contribution here.

His analysis started with a request in 1858 from Marx: "Can you tell me how often machinery has to be replaced in, say, your factory? Babbage maintains that in Manchester the bulk of machinery is renovated on average every five years.[72] This seems to me somewhat startling and not quite trustworthy. The average period for the replacement of machinery is *one* important factor in explaining the multi-year cycle which has been a feature of industrial development ever since the consolidation of big industry."[73]

Engels's well-reasoned reply confirmed Marx's scepticism: "Babbage's assertion is so absurd that were it true, England's industrial capital must continually diminish," considering that a five-year replacement period "would, of course, vastly increase the cost price of all articles – more, almost, than it would be increased by wages – in which case where is the advantage of machinery?" As for his own estimate, the "most reliable criterion is the percentage by which a manufacturer writes down his machinery each year for wear and tear and repairs, thus recovering the entire cost of his machines within a given period. This percentage is normally 7 1/2, in which case the machinery will be paid for over 13 1/3 years by an annual deduction from profits, i.e. will be replaceable without loss".

Drawing directly upon his own expertise in cotton manufacturing, Engels spelt out to Marx the difficulties in fixing upon a precise estimate and rejects the identification of the rate of economic depreciation with the rate at which machinery in the physical sense disappears from use:

"Now, 13 1/3 years is admittedly a long time in the course of which numerous bankruptcies and changes occur; you may enter other branches, sell your old machinery, introduce new improvements, but if this calculation wasn't more or less right, practice would have changed it long ago. Nor does the old machinery that has been sold promptly become old iron; it finds takers among the small spinners, etc., etc., who continue to use it. We ourselves have machines in operation that are certainly 20 years old and, when one occasionally takes a glance inside some of the more ancient and ramshackle concerns up here, one can see antiquated stuff that must be 30 years old at least. Moreover, in the case of most machines, only a few of the components wear out to the extent that they have to be replaced after 5 or 6 years. And even after 15 years, provided the basic principle of a machine has not been superseded by new inventions, there is relatively little difficulty in replacing worn out parts (I refer here to spinning and flyer frames), so that it is hard to set a definite term on the effective life of such machinery. Again, over the last 20 years improvements in spinning machinery have not been such as to preclude the incorporation of almost all of them in the existing *structure* of the machines, since nearly all are minor innovations. (Admittedly, in the case of carding, the enlargement of the carding cylinder was a major improvement which supplanted the old machines where *good* qualities were concerned, but for ordinary qualities the old machinery will be perfectly adequate for a long time yet)."

Marx replied: "My best thanks for your *'eclaircissements'* about machinery. The figure of 13 years corresponds closely enough to the theory, since it establishes a *unit* for one epoch of industrial reproduction which *plus ou moins* coincides with the period in which major crises recur; needless to say their course is also determined by factors of a quite different kind, depending on their period of reproduction. For me, the important thing is to discover in the immediate postulates of big industry one factor that determines cycles".[74]

So Engels provided Marx with at least an initial explanation of cycles in capitalist accumulation and production that he was searching for. When he was writing up Capital in 1865, he wrote to Engels that "you know, for reasons that I have not now to explain, capitalist production moves through certain periodical cycles". And in Volume 2 of Capital, edited by Engels, Marx wrote that "the cycle of related turnovers, extending over a number of years, within which capital is confined by its fixed component, is one of material foundations for the periodic cycle (crisis)… crisis is always the starting point of a large volume of investment . It is also therefore, if we consider society as a whole, more or less, the new basis for the next turnover cycle."

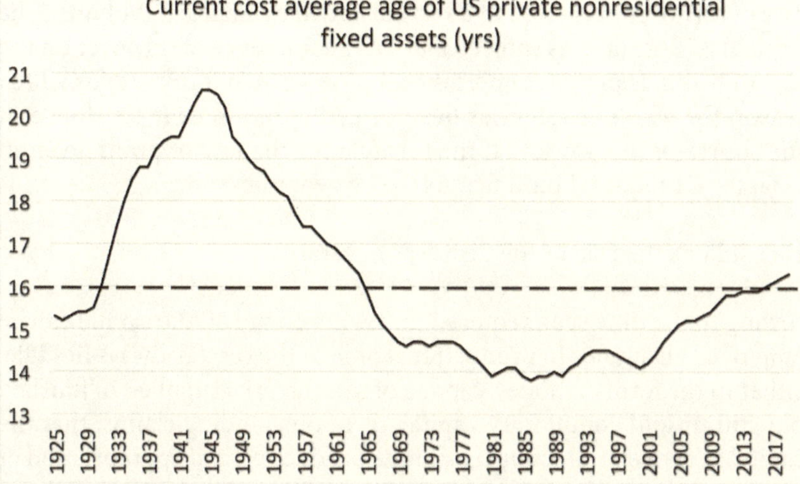

Was Engels (and Marx) right about the importance of the turnover of fixed capital in cycles in capitalist accumulation and was Engels right about their average duration in modern capitalism? In my book, The Long Depression, I show that the US Bureau of Economic Analysis provided data on the age structure of fixed capital assets in US industry. It averaged about 15-17 years in turnover (excluding the war years).[75]

The other key aspect of Engels work on the turnover of capital was the relation between turnover and the rate of profit. Here Engels is referring to the turnover of circulating capital (raw materials and inputs for production) not fixed assets as in his discussion with Marx above. Marx's law of profitability starts from the premise that value is only created by human labour power. If investment in the means of production rises more than investment in human labour power, then the rate of profit will tend to fall. And that indeed is what happens because investment in new technology is generally labour-shedding (as Engels argued in his Condition – see Chapter 3). But there are several counteracting factors that can arrest or curb the tendency for the rate to fall, in particular, an increase in the rate of surplus value (more profit versus wages) and the falling price of machinery lowering its costs.

Engels added another factor that Marx had neglected, changes in the rate of turnover of capital. In a section added by Engels in Volume 3, he explains: "But since its subject-matter, the influence of turnover on the rate of profit, is of vital importance, I have written it myself, for which reason the whole chapter has been placed in brackets. It developed in the course of this work that the formula for the rate of profit given in Chapter III required modification to be generally valid."

He explains the role of the turnover of capital.

"owing to the time span required for turnover, not all the capital can be employed all at once in production; some of the capital always lies idle, either in the form of money-capital, of raw material supplies, of finished but still unsold commodity-capital, or of outstanding claims; that the capital in active production, i.e., in the production and appropriation of surplus-value, is always short by this amount, and that the produced and appropriated surplus-value is always curtailed to the same extent. The shorter the period of turnover, the smaller this idle portion of capital as compared with the whole, and the larger, therefore, the appropriated surplus-value, provided other conditions remain the same…since the rate of profit only expresses the relation of the produced quantity of surplus-value to the total capital employed in its production, it is evident that any such reduction increases the rate of profit."

Engels then discusses ways in which the turnover of capital can be increased, particularly the speeding up of communications: "The chief means of reducing the time of circulation is improved communications. The period of turnover of the total world commerce has been reduced to the same extent, and the efficacy of the capital involved in it has been more than doubled or trebled. It goes without saying that this has not been without effect on the rate of profit."

In the 21st century, we can argue that speedier turnover from time and motion, internet demand and delivery helps reduce the costs of circulating capital and increases production within an amount of fixed capital. As Engels put it: "The direct effect of a reduced period of turnover on the production of surplus-value, and consequently of profit, consists of an increased efficiency imparted thereby to the variable portion of capital."

Engels provides some arithmetical examples to show how "the quantity of surplus-value appropriated in one year is therefore equal to the quantity of surplus-value appropriated in one turnover of the variable capital multiplied by the number of such turnovers per year." Thus "to make the formula precise for the annual rate of profit, we must substitute the annual rate of surplus-value for the simple rate of surplus-value, that is, substitute S' or s'n for s'. In other words, we must multiply the rate of surplus-value s', or, what amounts to the same thing, the variable capital v contained in C, by n, the number of turnovers of this variable capital in one year. We obtain $p' = s'n (v/C)$, which is the formula for the annual rate of profit."

The question of the role of turnover in affecting the rate of profit remains a matter of debate among Marxist economists. Peter Jones points out that there are three factors that have a direct effect on the rate of profit: a changing rate of surplus value; changing turnover time of variable capital, and a changing value composition of capital. An increase in the rate of surplus value or the number of turnovers of variable capital in a year leads to an increase in the rate of profit, while an increase in the VCC leads to a decrease in the rate of profit.[76]

Brian Green provides a unique method for measuring the turnover of capital, which he argues is essential to calculate in order to obtain an accurate measure of the rate of profit in Marxian terms.[77] Studies by Maito and by Carchedi and Roberts recognise the role of turnover in circulating capital (both constant and variable), but conclude that it is not that decisive in altering the trend in the rate of profit. An increased turnover will counteract the downward tendency of the rate of profit to fall but it will not reverse that direction, the evidence shows.[78] That result would be expected by Engels.

Engels on underconsumption and overproduction
In defence of Marx's law of profitability, Engels was always keen to refute alternative theories of crises, in particular, the theory that crises are caused by the underconsumption of the masses. In this theory, workers' wages are not enough to buy all the goods produced by capitalists and so there is a chronic lack of 'effective demand' that leads to the breakdown of production and investment.

There is some ambiguity in Marx's view on the underconsumption theory of crises. The usual quote from Marx to justify that he favoured the underconsumption theory is this. In Volume 3 of Capital, Marx says: "The ultimate reason for all real crises always remains the poverty and restricted consumption of the masses as opposed to the drive of capitalist production to develop the productive forces as though only the absolute consuming power of society constituted their limit."

But in a note in Volume 2 of Capital, Marx decisively rejects the underconsumption theory.

"It is sheer tautology to say that crises are caused by the scarcity of effective consumption ... That commodities are unsaleable means only that no effective purchasers have been found for them ... " (Capital, Vol. II, pp.410-11).

He continues:

"But if one were to attempt to give this tautology the semblance of a profounder justification by saying that the working class receives too small a portion of its own product and the evil would be remedied as soon as it receives a larger share of it and its wages increase in consequence, one could only remark that crises are always prepared by precisely a period in which wages rise generally and the working class actually gets a larger share of that part of the annual product which is intended for consumption. From the point of view of these advocates of sound and 'simple' (!) common sense, such a period should rather remove the crisis."

Engels always clearly rejected the underconsumption theory. In his book, Anti-Duhring, he takes on Dr Eugen Dühring[79] who borrowed the "under-consumptionist" explanation of crises. Anti-Duhring was written by Engels, but the completed drafts were read and approved, by Marx, who also contributed a whole section to it. While Engels concentrated on philosophy, history and science, it was Marx himself, as Engels admitted, who wrote a long section on economic theory in Anti-Dühring.

Engels points out: "Rodbertus took it from Sismondi, and Herr Dühring has in turn copied it, in his usual vulgarizing fashion, from Rodbertus." In Anti-Duhring, Engels points in his text to the current (1877) stagnation of the cotton industry as evidence against Rodbertus: "it requires a strong dose of deep-rooted effrontery to explain the present complete stagnation in the yarn and cloth markets by the under-consumption of the English masses and not by the over-production carried on by the English cotton-mill owners." And he referred to Marx's note in Volume 2 that it was "*ad notam* for possible followers of the Rodbertian theory of crises."

Engels goes on. "Unfortunately, the under-consumption of the masses, the restriction of the consumption of the masses to what is necessary for their maintenance and reproduction, is not a new phenomenon. It has existed as long as there have been exploiting and exploited classes. Even in those periods of history when the situation of the masses was particularly favourable, as for example in England in the 15th century, they under-consumed. They were very far from having their own annual total product at their disposal to be consumed by them. Therefore, while under-consumption has been a constant feature in history for thousands of years, the general shrinkage of the market which breaks out in crises as the result of a surplus of production is a phenomenon only of the last 50 years; and so Herr Dühring's whole superficial vulgar economics is necessary in order to explain the new collision not by the *new* phenomenon of over-production but by the thousand-year-old phenomenon of under-consumption. It is like a mathematician attempting to explain the variation in the ratio between two quantities, one constant and one variable, not by the variation of the variable but by the fact that the constant quantity remains unchanged."

Engels concludes: "The under-consumption of the masses is a necessary condition of all forms of society based on exploitation, consequently also of the capitalist form; but it is the capitalist form of production which first gives rise to crises. The under-consumption of the masses is therefore also a prerequisite condition of crises and plays in them a role which has long been recognised. But it tells us just as little why crises exist today as why they did not exist before."

Exactly - there is always under-consumption of the masses in all modes of production, but it does not explain the recurrent crises of investment and production under the capitalist mode for that very reason.

Unfortunately, versions of underconsumption theory remains dominant among Marxist economists. That's probably because the theorists of the Marxist Second International of social democratic parties relied on their economic theory from Volume One of Capital and generally did not digest Volume 2 which became available only in 1885 and Volume 3 in 1894 just before Engels' death. By then, they were wedded to the underconsumption theory – as it allowed some to take a reformist line on a socialist programme (just raise wages), as with the German social democrat leaders, Karl Kautsky[80] or Eduard Bernstein[81]; or even a radical line (breakdown was inevitable because of the 'lack of demand') as with Rosa Luxemburg. [82]

Engels draws the clear distinction between "under-consumption" (which has always existed in class society as a result of the poverty of the masses) and the phenomenon of overproduction, which is applicable to capitalism alone. But does that mean Marx and Engels had a theory of 'overproduction' in crises in which the law of profitability played no role? I think not.

Overproduction of commodities is the result of the overaccumulation of capital, which in turn comes about when the return on that capital falls to the point that accumulation stops. In Volume 3 of Capital, Marx put it: "overproduction of capital, not of individual commodities (although overproduction of commodities always includes overproduction of capital) is therefore simply overaccumulation of capital…because the purpose of capitalist production is the self-expansion of capital (ie the appropriation of surplus labour, the production of surplus value, of profit".[83]

Overproduction, the term often used by Engels and Marx to describe the cause of crises under capitalism arises because of the overproduction or overaccumulation of capital, means of production and labour relative to the profit created and appropriated: "even under the extreme conditions assumed by us this absolute over-production of capital is not absolute over-production, not absolute over-production of means of production. It is over-production of means of production only in so far as the latter serve as capital". So the contradiction between production and consumption under capitalism arises because of the tendency of the rate of profit on capital to fall, leading to an over-accumulation of capital. "Since the aim of capital is not to minister to certain wants, but to produce profit, and since it accomplishes this purpose by methods which adapt the mass of production to the scale of production, not vice versa, a rift must continually ensue between the limited dimensions of consumption under capitalism and a production which forever tends to exceed this immanent barrier."

It's not a lack of consumption that causes crises and it is not overproduction of commodities, but over-accumulation of capital, the specific form of capitalist crises. "If it is finally said that the capitalists have only to exchange and consume their commodities among themselves, then the entire nature of the capitalist mode of production is lost sight of; and also forgotten is the fact that it is a matter of expanding the value of the capital, not consuming it. ….The contradiction of the capitalist mode of production, however, lies precisely in its tendency towards an absolute development of the productive forces, which continually come into conflict with the specific conditions of production in which capital moves, and alone can move." Remember that Engels not only read these passages from Marx but also edited them, so if he disagreed, he had ample opportunity to show why.

Modern empirical work confirms that it is not the lack of consumption or low wages that leads to slumps; but on the contrary up to the point of the slump in production, consumption remains strong and wages can even be rising. It's investment that collapses, leading to a reduction in employment and then incomes and spending. And investment falls because at a certain point, profitability of capital has dropped to the point where total profits have slowed or even turned down, forcing a stoppage in business investment.[84]

Engels distorted Marx's law?

Despite this clear unity between Marx and Engels on crisis theory and the role of profitability, many Marxists continue to claim that Marx did not have a profitability theory of crises and had even dropped the law of profitability.

This brings us to the vexed question that appears to dominate the views of the modern scholars of Marx and Engel writings, namely the charge that Engels, in editing Volume 3 of Capital which contains Marx's law of the tendency of the rate of profit to fall, misunderstood and even distorted Marx's law, making it much more important than Marx ever intended. Indeed, it is argued by these modern scholars that Marx had dropped the law by the 1870s as being irrelevant to modern capitalism or to crises in capitalism. So Engels should never have included the three chapters on the law in Volume Three, let alone editing Marx's notes in such a way as to distort Marx's words.

This view is prominent among what are called the Neue Lekture (New Reading) School of Marx.[85] German Marxist scholar, Michael Heinrich has been the strongest supporter of this view. Author of an analysis of Marx's Capital, Heinrich has called for a return to the original material and the 'decanonisation' of the Engels version: "Engels's edition can no longer be considered to be volume III of Marx's *Capital;* it is not Marx's text 'in the full genuineness of his own presentation,' as Engels claimed in the supplement, but a strong editing of this presentation, a pre-interpreted textbook edition of Marx's manuscript. . . . [T]he text he presented is by no means the third volume of *Capital.* Every future discussion of Marx's economic theory will have to refer back to Marx's original manuscript"[86] But Heinrich goes further: "But even this manuscript [of 1864–5] also cannot simply be considered to be the third volume of *Capital.* . . . Marx was nowhere near solving all the *conceptual* problems" (1996: 465).

Regina Roth takes a similar position[87]: "One of the conclusions that these papers justify is that none of these Marx texts gives a systematic and concise presentation of his thought. He did not decide which of his various ways of treating the issues was the 'right' one; therefore, an 'authorized version,' in terms of an editor, does not really exist. There are merely fragments available. Thus . . . none of them can offer us a systematic presentation of what he thought" Similarly, Vollgraf and Jungnickel[88], following an account of Engels's interventions, refer to "the old dogma of the unity of Marx–Engels thought" concluding that "it is clear that Marx was in the midst of an open-ended process of research fermenting over many pages. It is also evident that his original text is at variance with various chords first struck by Engels's edition of 1894 which then continued to resonate down through the history of its influence" Finally, most recently, Musto has written of "[t]he intense editing activity on which Engels focused his efforts in the period between 1885–1914 [which] resulted in a transition from a very rough text, mainly comprising 'thoughts recorded *in statu nascendi*' and preliminary notes, to an organic text of systematic theory," and which "[n]ot surprisingly . . . resulted in many errors of interpretation"[89] And so it goes on.

It's true that Engels had a real task on his hands in editing Marx's scrawled writings into Volume 3. As he said in the preface: "At last I have the privilege of making public this third book of Marx's main work, the conclusion of the theoretical part. When I published the second volume, in 1885, I thought that except for a few, certainly very important, sections the third volume would probably offer only technical difficulties. This was indeed the case. But I had no idea at the time that these sections, the most important parts of the entire work, would give me as much trouble as they did, just as I did not anticipate the other obstacles, which were to retard completion of the work to such an extent. Next and most important of all, it was my eye weakness which for years restricted my writing time to a minimum, and which, even now, permits me to write by artificial light only in exceptional cases."

It was rumoured that Engels had to rub cocaine into his eyes in order to keep going on the edit. I personally sympathise with Engels here in writing this short book when he says: "When a man is past seventy, his Meynert's association fibres of the brain function with annoying prudence. He no longer surmounts interruptions in difficult theoretical problems as easily and quickly as before. It came about therefore that the work of one winter, if it was not completed, had to be largely begun anew the following winter. This was the case with the most difficult fifth part."

In sum, Engels reckoned that "the third volume was essentially different from that of editing the second. In the case of the third volume there was nothing to go by outside a first extremely incomplete draft. The beginnings of the various parts were, as a rule, pretty carefully done and even stylistically polished. But the farther one went, the more sketchy and incomplete was the manuscript, the more excursions it contained into arising side-issues whose proper place in the argument was left for later decision, and the longer and more complex the sentences, in which thoughts were recorded in *statu nascendi*.

"I began my work by dictating into readable copy the entire manuscript, which was often hard to decipher even for me. This alone required considerable time. It was only then that I could start on the actual editing. Engels proposed that: "Wherever my alterations or additions exceeded the bounds of editing, or where I had to apply Marx's factual material to independent conclusions of my own, if even as faithful as possible to the spirit of Marx, I have enclosed the entire passage in brackets and affixed my initials."

Heinrich argues that Marx probably dropped the law as being useful in any way in the 1870s when he too found it illogical and irrelevant to crises. And he never referred to it again up to his death in any discussion of the causes of the slumps that took place in those years.

Heinrich argues that after 1865 "Although Marx no longer made explicit reference to the" law of the downward trend of profit rates ", strong evidence suggests that Marx no longer supported this law. " And yet in his preface to Volume 3, Engels notes that Marx spent some considerable time looking at the relation of the rate of profit to the rate of surplus value in the 1870s (in contradiction to the claim that he had given up on the law). "The entire mathematical calculation of the relation between the rate of surplus-value and the rate of profit (which makes up our Chapter III) is introduced in the very beginning. There was a series of uncompleted mathematical calculations for Chapter III, as well as a whole, almost complete, notebook dating from the seventies, which presents the relation of the rate of surplus value to the rate of profit in the form of equations. My friend Samuel Moore . . . undertook to edit this notebook for me, a work for which he was far better equipped, being an old Cambridge mathematician. It was from his summary, with occasional use of the main manuscript, that I then compiled Chapter III."

This explanation is further elaborated in an important footnote at the close of the chapter itself, describing a specific omission from the notebook: The manuscript contains also very detailed calculations of the difference between the rate of surplus value and the rate of profit (s_-p_-), which has very interesting peculiarities, and whose movement indicates where the two rates draw apart or approach one another. These movements may also be represented by curves. But Engels decided not to produce this material in Volume 3, "because it is of less importance to the immediate purposes of this work." So Engels excluded Marx's mathematical work on the rate of profit from Volume 3, even though it would have supported the view that Marx still held to the law.

Back in 1978, Jerrold Seigel[90] had a look at the manuscripts. Yes, Engels made significant editorial changes to Marx's writings on the law as in Capital Volume 3. He divided Marx's text into three chapters 13- 15; 13 was the law; 14 was counteracting influences and 15 described the internal contradictions. In doing so, Engels shifted some of the text into Chapter 13 on 'the law as such' when in fact in Marx's manuscript, the words came after the counteracting factors in Chapter 14. But in this way, Engels actually makes it appear that Marx balances the counter-tendencies in equal measure with the law as such, when the original order of the text re-emphasises the law <u>after</u> talking about counter influences. So, as Seigel puts it: "Engels made Marx's confidence in the actual operation of the profit law seem weaker than Marx's manuscript indicates it to be." This is hardly an edit that suggests Engels was determined to defend a law that Marx had dropped.

While some 6-8 percent of Marx's text of Capital 3 is actually by Engels, 90 percent of the interpolations – "from the tiniest scrap of a sentence to entire chapters" – are "marked" as such, according to Vollgraf and Jungnickel. This datum suggests that Engels was certainly not engaged in a deliberate campaign to mislead readers as to authorship. Fred Moseley recently introduced a new translation into English of Marx's four drafts for Volume 3 of Capital by Regina Roth, where Marx's law of profitability is developed and shows how Engels edited those drafts for Capital[91]. Moseley shows that much maligned Engels did a solid job of interpreting Marx's drafts and there was no real distortion. "One can, therefore, surmise that Engels' interventions were made on the basis that he wished to make Marx's statements appear sharper and thus more useful for contemporary political and societal debate, for instance, in the third chapter, on the tendency of the rate of profit to fall."

Indeed, one powerful argument in favour of Engels' edit of the law in Volume 3, is that it closely follows Marx's notes found in the Grundrisse written in 1857–8 and not seen by Engels. Grundrisse provides independent evidence of the major progress already made by Marx in the late 1850s and supports the veracity of the Engels version, including his representation of the very high significance for Marx of the profit-rate trend – considered by Marx in 1857–8 as "one of the most striking phenomena of modern production."

From 1870, Engels had retired and moved from Manchester to London, so Marx and he met together as a matter of routine, usually daily. Discussions could go on into the small hours. Marx's house lay little more than 10 minutes walk away and there was always the Mother Redcap or the Grafton Arms. If Marx had really dropped the law that he had developed and promoted for over 20 years, he surely would have informed Engels. Seigel also points out that the chapter written by Engels on "The Effect of Turnover on the Rate of Profit" (see above) would hardly have been done if Engels thought Marx had dropped the law anyway.

Writing to Sombart in March 1895, Engels insisted that Capital 3 presented the work of Marx faithfully: "I must . . . thank you for the high esteem in which you must hold me if you take the view that I could have turned Volume III into something better than it is. But I am unable to share that opinion and believe I have done my duty by presenting Marx in Marx's own words, even at the risk of expecting the reader to do rather more thinking for himself."

In his Supplement, written from May to June 1895, Engels explains that in editing Volume 3 he had sought "to produce as authentic a text as possible, to demonstrate the new results obtained by Marx in Marx's own words as far as possible, to intervene myself only where absolutely unavoidable, and even then to leave the reader in no doubt as to who was talking to him. The scope of his "intervention", said Engels, was limited "to eliminate difficulties in understanding, to bring more to the fore important aspects whose significance is not strikingly enough evident in the text, and to make some important additions to the text written in 1865 to fit the state of affairs in 1895." So in 1895, Engels still saw the relevance of Marx's law of profitability and thought Marx would have done also.

Engels develops cycle theory

In the Condition, Engels adopted a cyclical dimension to changes in the economy namely recurring industrial crises with a degree of regularity. The coincidence of cyclical movement across industries is attributed to "the centralising tendency of competition, which drives the hands thrown out of one branch into such other branches as are most easily accessible, and transfers the goods which cannot be disposed of in one market to other markets," a tendency that "has gradually brought the single minor crises nearer together and united them into one period-ically recurring crisis. Such a crisis usually recurs once in five years after a brief period of activity and general prosperity; the home market, like all foreign ones, is glutted with English goods, which it can only slowly absorb."

Engels had developed the concept of cycles of boom and slump in emerg-ing industrial capitalism from observation. But also he relied on the work of Sismondi who had also taken note of the increasing concentration of capital and recurring trade cycles. Engels, though, specifically expressed his indebtedness to John Wade regarding the periodicity of cycles as integral to the capitalist process.[92] The worsening of the endogenous cycle with an expansion of the range of activities subject to cyclical pressures does not, however, derive from Wade. Nevertheless, Wade does write regarding "commercial depression and prosperity" that "[b]anking and the introduction of paper currency, may have increased their intensity, and caused them to alternate in shorter periods".

Engels reckoned that crises, described in terms of 'periodic overpro-duction', were a result of the industrial revolution: "In the steam-engine and the other machines large-scale industry created the means of increasing industrial production in a short time and at slight expense to an unlimited extent....The result was that the goods manufactured could not be sold, and a so-called trade crisis ensued. Factories had to stand idle, factory owners went bankrupt, and the workers lost their bread....After a while the surplus products were sold, the factories started working again, wages went up, and gradually business was more brisk than ever."

In the Condition, he delivers a graphic description of depression entailing general glut, bankruptcies, plant shutdowns, part-time work and layoffs, depletion of accumulated savings, falling wages, and pressure on poor relief. "The most depressed period," Engels adds, "is brief, lasting, at worst, but one, two, or two and a half years". So 'normal' recessions or slumps last a year or two before business picks up again – again a clear identification of the length of slumps that has lasted until now. Leaning on the observations of these other authors, Engels notes the coincidence of cycles across industries.

Looking back to that early period of the English industrial revolution in the 1887 American edition of the Condition, and also in the prefaces to the English edition and the Second German edition of 1892 of the Condition, Engels referred to "[t]he recurring period of the great industrial crisis...stated in the text as five years. This was the period apparently indicated by the course of events from 1825 to 1842. But the industrial history from 1842 to 1868 has shown that the real period is one of ten years; that the intermediate revolutions were secondary and tended more and more to disappear."

Engels adopted the idea of cyclical crises on the empirical evidence – the theoretical explanation comes with Marx in Capital and later. Marx thought there were cycles in capitalism: "Once the cycle begins, it is regularly repeated. Effects, in their turn, become causes, and the varying accidents of the whole process, which always reproduces its own conditions, take on the form of periodicity"[93]

Marx spent some considerable time and research in trying to identify cycles in the capitalist economy.[94] He particularly looked for periodicity in cycles. Right up to the end of his research on the capitalist economy, Marx continued to look for cyclical movements. He wrote to Engels in

May 1873 about "a problem which I have been wrestling with in private for a long tim[e]." He had been examining "tables which give prices, discount rate, etc. etc. . . . I have tried several times—for the analysis of crises—to calculate these ups and downs as irregular curves, and thought (I still think that it is possible with enough tangible material) that I could determine the main laws of crises mathematically."[95]

Marx saw the immobility of fixed capital as a part of the explanation of the periodicity of the cycle. This relates to the discussion (see above) that he had with Engels on the turnover of fixed capital. Marx thought that the duration of the accumulation cycle (boom and slump) was about five to seven years, a view he revised to ten years when the expected crisis did not strike in 1852. So Marx developed the idea that the cycle was connected with the replacement of fixed capital. On this basis, he argued, "there can be no doubt at all that the cycle through which industry has been passing in *plus ou moins* ten-year periods since the large-scale development of fixed capital, is linked with the total reproduction phase of capital determined in this way. We shall find other determining factors too, but this is one of them."[96]

As mentioned above, Engels told Marx that it was normal to set aside 7.5 percent for depreciation, which implied a replacement cycle of thirteen years, although he noted twenty- and thirty-year-old machines still working.[97] Marx considered that "So far the period of these cycles has been ten or twelve years, but there is no reason to consider this a constant figure." Indeed, he thought that the cycle of replacement capital would shorten. Later Engels began to argue that "the acute form of the periodic process, with its former ten-year cycle, appears to have given way to a more chronic, long drawn out, alternation between a relatively short and slight business improvement and a relatively long, indecisive depression—taking place in the various industrial countries at different times."[98] So the cycle could be longer than ten to thirteen years.

Engels' measure of the length of cycles in British capitalism was very accurate. A recent study by the Bank of England found that the cycles of boom and slump in the early 19th century were "between two and five years". Later in the century recessions were rarer, occurring around every eight years.[99]

In modern Marxist political economy, some authors have attempted to integrate a theory of crises under capitalism with their regularity and recurrence.[100]

Engels on 'fictitious capital' and 'financialisation'

In a startingly contemporary account of the cycle of boom and slump, in the Condition, Engels anticipates Marx: "Then come the daring speculators working with fictitious capital, living upon credit, ruined if they cannot speedily sell; they hurl themselves into this universal, disorderly race for profits, multiply the disorder and haste by their unbridled passion, which drives prices and production to madness. It is a frantic struggle, which carries away even the most experienced and phlegmatic; goods are spun, woven, hammered, as if all mankind were to be newly equipped, as though two thousand million new consumers had been discovered in the moon."

So Engels was the first to use the Marxian political economy term of 'fictitious capital' in categorising speculative investment in credit and stocks which will soon be shown as fictitious when the slump comes. "All at once the shaky speculators abroad, who must have money, begin to sell, below market price of course, for their need is urgent; one sale is followed by others, prices fluctuate, speculators throw their goods upon the market in terror the market is disordered, credit shaken, one house after another stops payments, bankruptcy follows bankruptcy, and the discovery is made that three times more goods are on hand or under way than can be consumed." Engels concludes "This is the beginning of the crisis, which then takes precisely the same course as its predecessor and gives place in turn to a season of prosperity."

Looking back after Marx's death, Engels comments: "I noticed that in the 'forties already in Manchester, the London Stock Exchange reports were utterly useless for the course of industry and its periodical maxima and minima because these gentry tried to explain everything from crises on the money market, which were generally only symptoms. At that time, the object was to explain away the origin of industrial crises as temporary overproduction, so that the thing had in addition its tendentious side, provocative of distortion. This point has now gone (for us, at any rate, for good and all), added to which it is indeed a fact that the money market can also have its own crises, in which direct disturbances of industry only play a subordinate part or no part at all."

Engels developed this point about monetary crises. "As soon as trading in money becomes separate from trade in commodities it has (under certain conditions imposed by production and commodity trade and within these limits) a development of its own, special laws and separate phases determined by its own nature. If, in this further development, trade in money extends in addition to trade in securities and these securities are not only government securities but also industrial and transport stocks and shares, so that money trade conquers the direct control over a portion of the production by which, taken as a whole, it is itself controlled, then the reaction of money trading on production becomes still stronger and more complicated."

Then the role of 'fictitious capital' emerges. "The money traders have become the owners of railways, mines, iron works, etc. These means of production take on a double aspect if their working has to be directed sometimes in the immediate interests of production but sometimes also according to the requirements of the shareholders, in so far as they are money traders. The most striking example of this is the American railways, whose working is entirely dependent on the stock exchange operations of a Jay Gould or a Vanderbilt, etc., these having nothing whatever to do with the particular railway concerned and its interests as a means of communication. And even here in England we have seen struggles lasting for tens of years between different railway companies over the boundaries of their respective territories – struggles in which an enormous amount of money was thrown away, not in the interests of production and communications but simply because of a rivalry which usually only had the object of facilitating the stock exchange dealings of the shareholding money traders." So it is possible that "the movement of the industrial market is, in the main and with the reservations already indicated, reflected in the money market and, of course, in inverted form."

Here Engels discerns the rising role of finance capital in modern capitalism, presaging the modern 'financialisation' thesis that is so popular among heterodox and Marxist economists as an alternative to Marx's theory of crises. What this shows is that 'financialisation' was far from a new idea for the 20th century as claimed by its exponents.[101] In that sense, financialisation was 'nothing new under the sun'. [102]

But what is most important, Engels did not propose the two concepts proposed by modern financialisation theory that 1) finance is a second source of surplus value after production and that 2) financial excess is now the main cause of crises and not the excess of productive capital relative to profitability. Yes, money can become "separate from trade in commodities it has a development of its own, special laws and separate phases determined by its own nature", but only "under certain conditions imposed by production and commodity trade and within these limits."

Writing in Anti-Duhring, Engels expounds: "Political economy, in the widest sense, is the science of the laws governing the production and exchange of the material means of subsistence in human society. Production and exchange are two different functions. Production may occur without exchange, but exchange — being necessarily an exchange of products—cannot occur without production. Each of these two social functions is subject to the action of external influences which to a great extent are peculiar to it and for this reason each has, also to a great extent, its own special laws. But on the other hand, they constantly determine and influence each other to such an extent that they might be termed the abscissa and ordinate of the economic curve."

Later after Marx's death, Engels developed further this Marxist concept of fictitious capital, taking into account developments in finance capital in Britain and the US after Capital was written. Engels commented, "At that time [1865], the stock exchange was still a place where the capitalists took away each other's accumulated capital" Now it is otherwise," by virtue of its new role of encouraging "expansion of production.". A "change has taken place which today assigns a considerably increased and constantly growing role to the stock exchange, and which, as it develops, tends to concentrate all production, industrial as well as agricultural, and all commerce, the means of communication as well as the functions of exchange, in the hands of stock exchange operators, so that the stock exchange becomes the most prominent representative of capitalist production itself. The impact extended far and wide: "Now all foreign investments in the form of shares. To mention England alone: American railways, North and South, then colonisation. Today this is purely a subsidiary of the stock exchange, in whose interests the European powers divided Africa a few years ago."

The work of economic historians since bears out Engels' analysis of that contemporary period. Gareth Campbell notes that during the 1840s, Britain experienced two 'bubbles' and a financial crisis. Railway shares underwent a substantial price reversal during the Railway Mania, and the price of corn rose and fell dramatically soon afterwards. A period known as the Commercial Crisis then followed, which resulted in widespread company failures. These events occurred shortly after the introduction of the Bank Charter Act which resulted in a major reform of the monetary system.[103]

The British economy began the 1840s in a subdued condition, but from 1843 the economy recovered. The prices of railway shares then began to rise substantially and a large number of new railways were projected, during a period which has become known as the British Railway Mania. A market index of railway shares, suggests that, on average, railway share prices increased by 98.4 per cent between January 1843 and August 1845. However, prices then fell dramatically, by 18.2 per cent by the end of November 1845. After a brief recovery, prices continued to fall until April 1850, with a decline of 57.5 per cent from peak to trough. Engels arrived in England right in the middle of this speculative collapse.[104]

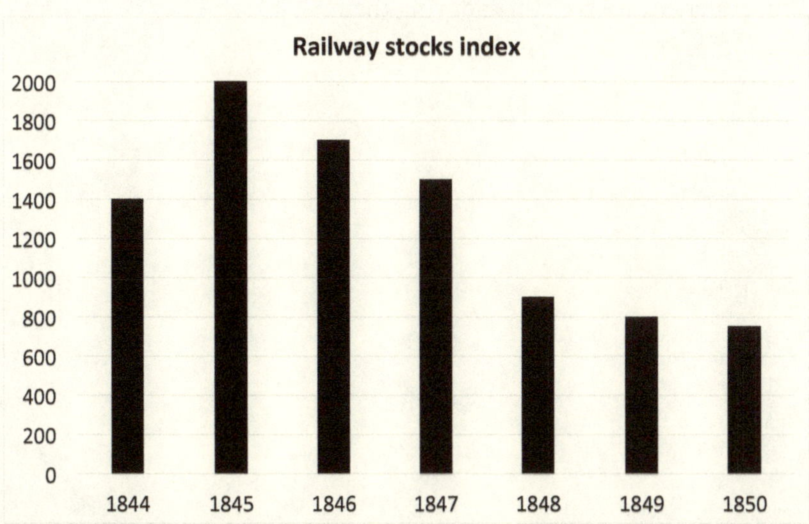

With collapsing railroad prices as background, the proximate cause of the commercial crisis of 1847 was the shock to the agricultural sector and the subsequent financial and monetary fallout. Both Ireland and England suffered massive harvest failures in 1846, which led to food shortages and drove up commodity prices. Aggravating the tightening monetary conditions was a rash of failures of "commercial" firms occasioned by failed speculative plays (via derivatives!) in foodstuffs, particularly corn. The deflating railway bubble, which bankrupted many enterprises and raised doubts about the stability of the financial system, set the stage for the panic.

Engels reckoned that regular crises could lay the basis for revolutionary ferment. "Thus since the beginning of this century the state of industry has continually fluctuated between periods of prosperity and periods of crisis, and almost regularly every five to seven years a similar crisis has occurred, and every time it has entailed the greatest misery for the workers, general revolutionary ferment, and the greatest danger to the entire existing system." Engels notes that "Commercial crises, the mightiest levers for all independent development of the proletariat, will probably shorten the process, acting in concert with foreign competition and the deepening ruin of the lower middle-class. I think the people will not endure more than one more crisis."

Unfortunately, we are still enduring them.

CHAPTER SIX

Engels after Marx

Having taken a back seat for most of the time while Marx wrote Capital, during the 1870s Engels began to produce various pamphlets and articles expounding and explaining Marxian political economy. And after Marx's death in 1883, Engels became the standard bearer for all that Marxism stood for. Having been a Marxist before Marx, he now became the Marxist after Marx.

As we have seen in the previous chapter, in the last ten years of his life, Engels edited the next two volumes of Capital and defended its arguments against all comers. But Engels also developed Marxist economics in those last years. The major capitalist economies of Europe and the US had entered what was eventually called the Great Depression, or later the 19th century Long Depression, which lasted, depending on the country, as it was not simultaneous, from about 1873 to 1897. During this period, there were alternating booms and slumps, but overall, the major economies experienced lower growth rates than in the boom upwave of 1850-1870 and the profitability of capital fell. Investment growth was weaker, unemployment generally higher, inflation weak (indeed deflation) and interest rates low.[105]

Engels on depression

Engels was well aware of these developments. In Anti-Duhring, he had revived his argument about the cyclical nature of crises under capitalism that he first raised in his Outline/Umrisse back in 1842: "As a matter of fact, since 1825, when the first general crisis broke out, the whole industrial and commercial world, production and exchange among all civilized peoples and their more or less barbaric hangers-on, are thrown out of joint about once every 10 years. Commerce is at a stand-still, the markets are glutted, products accumulate, as multitudinous as they are unsaleable, hard cash disappears, credit vanishes, factories are closed, the mass of the workers are in want of the means of subsistence, because they have produced too much of the means of subsistence; bankruptcy follows upon bankruptcy, execution upon execution. The stagnation lasts for years; productive forces and products are wasted and destroyed wholesale, until the accumulated mass of commodities finally filter off, more or less depreciated in value, until production and exchange gradually begin to move again. Little by little, the pace quickens. It becomes a trot. The industrial trot breaks into a canter, the canter in turn grows into the headlong gallop of a perfect steeplechase of industry, commercial credit, and speculation, which finally, after breakneck leaps, ends where it began — in the ditch of a crisis. And so over and over again."

Engels counted the crises. "We have now, since the year 1825, gone through this five times, and at the present moment (1877), we are going through it for the sixth time. And the character of these crises is so clearly defined that Fourier hit all of them off when he described the first "crise plethorique", a crisis from plethora."[106]

Engels' close study of the crises of 1866 and 1873 led him to alter his view that capitalism was subject to just short-length booms and slumps. Engels perceptively concluded in 1885, that "we have had, ever since 1876, a chronic state of stagnation in all dominant branches of industry. Neither will the full crash come; nor will the period of longed-for prosperity to which we used to be entitled before and after it. A dull depression, a chronic glut of all markets for all trades, that is what we have been living in for nearly ten years". This could have been written about the second decade of the 21st century.

In the preface to the first English edition of Capital Volume One (1886), Engels elaborated: "The decennial cycle of stagnation, prosperity, over-production and crisis, ever recurrent from 1825 to 1867, seems indeed to have run its course; but only to land us in the slough of despond of a permanent and chronic depression". Engels tentatively concluded that "perhaps it is only a matter of a prolongation of the duration of the cycle. In the early years of world commerce, 1815–47, it can be shown that these cycles lasted about five years; from 1847–67 the cycle is clearly ten years; is it possible that we are now in the preparatory stage of a new world crash of unparalleled vehemence?"

Engels' friend, German social democrat Eduard Bernstein rejected this view. In the 1890s, Bernstein argued that "[n]o signs of a worldwide economic crash of unprecedented violence have been detected, nor can the improvement of trade between crises be characterized as particularly short-lived"[107] Indeed, for Bernstein, the joint question arose, "(1) whether the enormous geographical expansion of the world market in conjunction with the extraordinary reduction in the time required for transport and the transmission of news have not so increased the possibilities of *levelling out* disturbances, and (2) whether the enormously increased wealth of the European industrial states in conjunction with the elasticity of the modern credit system and the rise of industrial cartels have not so limited the *reactive force* of local or individual disturbances on the general state of business that, at least for some time, general trade crises similar to the earlier ones are to be regarded as unlikely".

On the whole, Bernstein thought it was "impossible to decide a priori the ultimate relation of these forces to one another, or their development"; but "[u]nless unforeseen external events bring about a general crisis . . . there is no compelling reason to conclude, on purely economic grounds, that such a crisis is imminent. Local and partial recessions are unavoidable. Thanks to the present organisation and expansion of the world market, and thanks particularly to the great expansion in food production, a general stagnation is not unavoidable. Perhaps nothing has contributed so much to the mitigation of business crises, or to the prevention of their increase, as the fall in rents and food prices"

So was Engels right about a Long Depression starting in the 1870s? The debate on whether there was a depression has been lengthy since. Beales supported Engels: "the period embraces three slumps and two intervening recoveries. The peak of the good years was reached in 1872, and the succeeding slump lasted till 1879. Three years of improvement then followed. The second spasm of depression lasted from 1882 to 1886. It was succeeded by four years of recovery, after which the third phase of depression pursued its course, lasting from 1890 till 1896."[108] Hatton finds that "before 1914 there was a fairly regular cycle consistent with other cyclical indicators, with unemployment rates reaching 6 to 8 per cent in depressions and falling to 3 or 4 per cent in booms".[109] Saul notes that, extracting from cyclical variation, "[u]nemployment during 1874–95 was clearly higher than during 1851–73 and 1896–1914, the figures being 7.2 per cent compared with 5 per cent and 5.4 percent respectively."[110]

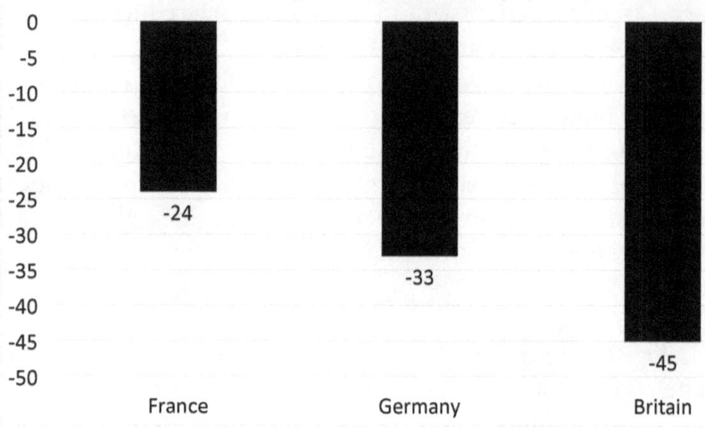

In my book, The Long Depression, I have discussed the arguments for and against the existence of a "permanent and chronic depression" from the 1870s, as claimed by Engels. The great leftist economist Arthur Lewis provides compelling evidence that Engels was right – at least for British capitalism. [111]. Lewis also shows that the main reason for the depression was the failure to restore the profitability of capital despite several slumps. Whereas profitability rose in Britain during the long boom of 1855 to 1871, it was followed by a down phase from 1871 to 1893. Lewis: "In the low level of profits in the last quarter of the century we have an explanation which is powerful enough to explain the retardation of industrial growth in the 1880s and 1890s."

Indeed, Engels' depression theory showed "some anticipation of Kondratieff's work on Long Cycles."[112] Under the Kondratieff theory, there are long cycles of upwave and downwave in capitalism. The first of such cycles begins with the emergence of industrial capitalism from about 1785 rising and then troughing in the early 1840s, the time of the Engels' pause (see chapter 3). The second cycle peaked in the last 1860s and reached a trough, depending on the country, in the mid-1880s or 1890s. The next cycle then peaked in 1920. So Engels' observation of a depression period from the 1870s up to his death in 1895 has support in the empirical evidence and in theory.[113]

Engels and the end of British hegemony
The long depression of 1873-97 brought about a shift in the economic power relations of the major economies. Well before the depression, Engels had been the first to argue that the United States would eventually surpass the industrial and trading strength of Britain, then basking in its status as the 'workshop of the world' in the 1850s and 1860s, when Marx wrote Capital. After the end of the civil war, US capitalism began to motor and, in the depression, the mature industrial power of Britain began to wane at least relatively, not only to the US, but also to Germany and France.

When in 1885, reviewing his early work The Condition, thus 40 years later, Engels wrote: "the manufacturing monopoly of England is the pivot of present social system, but even while it lasted , the markets could not keep pace with the increasing productivity of English manufacturers… so how will it be when Continental and especially American goods, flow in ever increasing quantities. So much for the universal panacea, free trade."

Thus, Engels points out that when a capitalist economy is dominant worldwide, it is in favour of free trade, as Britain was from the 1840s to 1870s. But free trade breeds rivals and after the experience of the

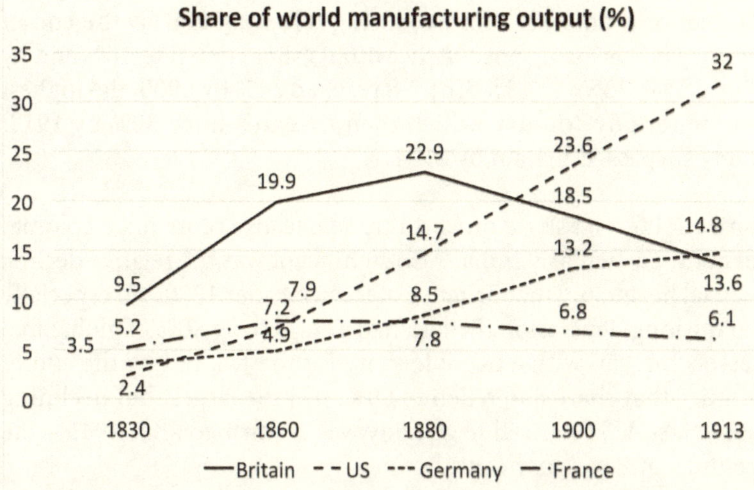

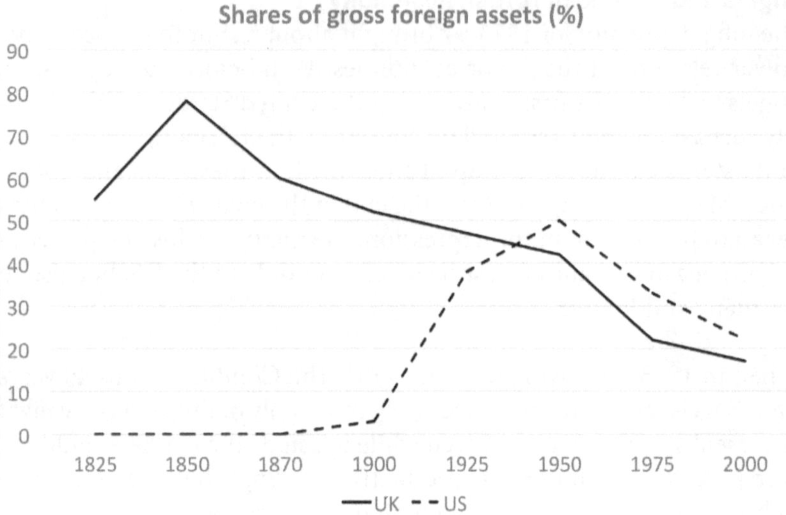

depression, British policy changed from 'free trade' to protectionist measures for its colonial empire. In 1860, when Marx was writing Capital, Britain had 20% of world manufacturing output compared to just 8% for France, 7% for the US, 5% for Germany. By 1880, when Engels had written Anti-Duhring, the British share had risen to nearly 23%, but the US share had more than doubled to 15% and Germany had passed that of France. Britain was losing relatively. But by the end of the century it was losing absolutely, with its share down to 18% and by the World War down to 13%. The US reached 24% by 1900, the highest ever share for any country, which then rose to a huge 32% by 1914. Germany surpassed Britain by 1914.

Britain sustained its share of world trade because of its huge colonial possessions, particularly India. Also significant was the relative decline in financial hegemony that Britain experienced after 1850 and especially during the long depression. Britain had a staggering 80% of global foreign assets in 1850 with a neglible share for the US. But by the end of the century that share had fallen to 50%, still the largest but declining as a share fast. US financial hegemony was confirmed after 1945 – the half century of Pax Americana.

Engels perceptively identified that the depression meant the breaking of the British hegemony. "England's monopoly of the world market is being increasingly shattered by the participation of France, Germany and, above all, of America in world trade, a new form of evening-out appears to come into operation."

In the Condition, just at the peak of British dominance, Engels makes a very early prediction that Britain will not be able to maintain its production and trade hegemony over other nations. "Britain's international competitiveness… decrees that England is to become a huge workshop for the world, although the mass of Americans, Germans and Belgians are ruining one market after another for the English by their competition." After all, Engels says "any country is adapted to holding a monopoly of manufacture, it is America. Should English manufacture be thus vanquished–and in the course of the next twenty years, if the present conditions remain unchanged, this is inevitable."

And even if Britain were to maintain its hegemony, it would be no way out for British capitalism. "But assuming that England retained the monopoly of manufactures, that its factories perpetually multiply, what must be the result? The commercial crises would continue, and grow more violent, more terrible, with the extension of industry and the multiplication of the proletariat. The proletariat would increase in geometrical proportion, in consequence of the progressive ruin of the lower middle-class and the giant strides with which capital is concentrating itself in the hands of the few; and the proletariat would soon embrace the whole nation, with the exception of a few millionaires." This is a lesson for now too. Even if the US were successful in weakening and curbing the rise of its major 21st century economic rival, China, that would not avoid crises of production and investment and the growing strength of the global proletariat.

The end of British hegemony revived the issue of whether Marxists should support 'free trade' or protection. In 1888, Engels reviewed Marx's position of the 1840s: "[B]ecause Free Trade is the natural, the normal atmosphere for this historical evolution" – the process described by Marx – "the economic medium in which the conditions for the inevitable social revolution will be the soonest created, – for this reason, and for this alone, did Marx declare in favour of Free Trade"[114]

Engels had rehearsed the theme in 1850[115]. He identified the "free trade" movement itself with the Manchester School (of 'free markets'), and he attributed to it the view that low earnings were essential for successful exportation and growth – essentially, one might say, a mercantilist position. He favoured free trade on Marx's ground that it allowed industrial capitalism the unhindered scope to destroy itself by overproducing in the face of limited markets, with the inevitable outcome –that is, increasingly severe cycles and ultimate collapse.

But by insisting on this feature, Engels implied that at other periods or places the same objective might not justify free trade. In a letter to German Social Democrat, August Bebel[116] in 1892, Engels remarks that "unemployment [in Germany] might well get worse next year. For protectionism has had exactly the same effect as free trade – the flooding of individual national markets and this almost everywhere, although it's not so bad over here as where you are."

For Engels, the question of free trade or protection depended on what was in the interests of workers. In emerging American capitalism, there was a case for protection. "it is also the only good aspect of protectionism – at any rate in the case of most of the continental countries and of America. Large-scale industry, big capitalists and large masses of proletarians are being artificially nurtured, the centralisation of capital is being speeded up and the middle classes destroyed." On the other hand, protection was no good if it stopped an economy from becoming competitive in world markets. And that would soon be the case for both America and Germany, once they had the edge over Britain. Then "protective tariffs are now simply a hindrance because they hinder those countries from taking their proper place in the world market. In America, therefore, they are bound to be abandoned before long and Germany is bound to follow suit."

The hegemonic power is always in favour of free trade – no tariffs or regulations etc. And indeed, in periods of healthy capitalist growth, globalisation of trade (and capital flows accelerates), as in the period 1850-70 and later from mid-1890s, and of course from 1980s. But in periods of depression, then protectionism becomes the cry, particularly if the hegemonic power is under threat, as was Britain from the 1890s or the US now. Engels regarded protection as the policy of "every industrial country," adopted in "general chronic overproduction, depressed prices, falling and even wholly disappearing profits." And so it proved particularly in the Great Depression of the 1930.

The European Union is a good example of how free trade can benefit capitalist economies in periods of healthy capitalist expansion, but then become an iniquitous destruction of weaker economies when depression is the order of the day. To begin with, the EU enabled some 'convergence' in productivity and per capita incomes through the late 1990s, but once the euro project began, divergence set in, especially in the Long Depression after 2009.[117]. For Engels, from labour's point of view, supporting free trade or protection was not one of principle, but of practice.

Engels on imperialism and war

Indeed, it was falling profitability and increased rivalry between the major capitalist powers during the late 19th century depression that led to the rise of imperialism and the attempt to counteract falling profitability through the exploitation of the existing colonies of the major European powers. This was the rise of modern imperialism.[118] Those countries without colonies had to adopt an aggressive attitude towards those that did ie Germany versus France and Britain.

The UK rate of profit 1855-1900 %

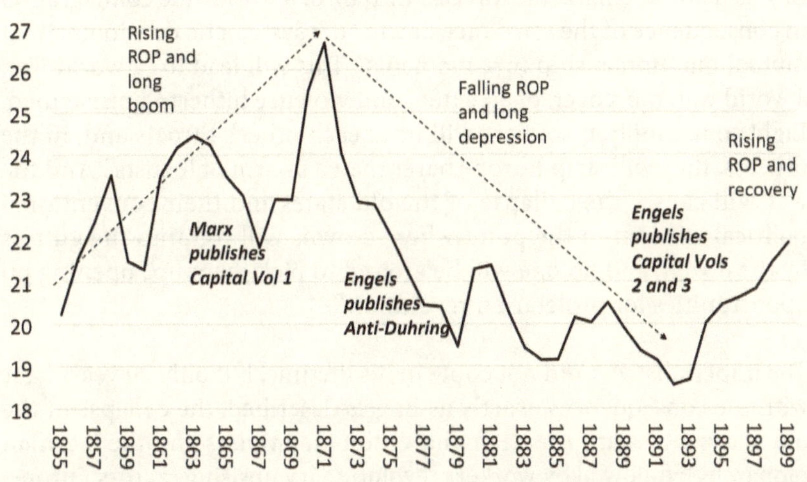

The UK rate of profit had risen sharply from 1855 to 1871 (30%), in the period of the long boom. But then it fell sharply in the Long Depression to a low in the mid-1880s (-22%), which was not really overcome until the mid-1890s (17%).

The issues of imperialist appropriation of value from the periphery, and whether workers are incorporated into imperialism are again topical. Engels also considered the issue of whether tribute from the colonies had enabled British imperialism to buy off a section of the English working class – what Lenin later called the 'labour aristocracy'. "The English working class have to a certain extent shared in the benefits of the monopoly. These benefits were very unequally parcelled out amongst them; the privileged minority pocketed most, but even the great mass had at least a temporary share now and then."

But the end of British hegemony would alter that. "With the breakdown of that monopoly the English working class will lose that privileged position; it will find itself generally–the privileged and leading minority not excepted – on a level with its fellow-workers abroad. And that is the reason why there will be Socialism again in England." Engels forecast the rise of the British Labour party in gaining the ear and the vote of the majority of British workers in the post-depression years, based on the rise of the new unions based on unskilled workers in new industries.

Engels made a remarkable forecast in 1887 of a worldwide conflagration in consequence of the arms race due to "the systematic development of mutual one-upmanship in armaments". This will lead to "a world war, a world war, moreover, of an extent and violence hitherto unimagined. Eight to ten million soldiers will be at each other's throats and, in the process, they will strip Europe barer than a swarm of locusts". And the war will cause "the collapse of the old states and their conventional political wisdom to the point where crowns will roll into the gutters by the dozen, and no one will be around to pick them up", opening up opportunities for proletarian revolution."

The imperialist war did not come in his lifetime, but only 20 years later with the consequences exactly as Engels described: the collapse of the old states (Russian, Austrian and Ottoman empires and the German monarchy); followed by workers revolutionary uprisings across Europe.

In 1885, he wrote that a European war was a serious possibility because of the battle among imperialist powers over control of the Balkans. Again, Engels' prescience was spot on – the Great War sparked by the assassination of the heir to the Austrian Empire in Sarajevo. Such a war, Engels said, would halt the progress of the labour movement and possibly condemn it to the backburner in history, causing bloodshed and devastation followed by a collapsed world economy. Again, he was right: the international labour movement capitulated to nationalism and subsumed itself to the imperialist war.

Engels estimated that the cost of the war would be one trillion francs and over 1 and half million lives. He understated that. He expected the war to last a long time and cause destruction not seen before – a prediction much more accurate than the initial claim of the imperialist governments that the war would be over in weeks.

Engels spelt out the horrors ahead. "Eight to ten million soldiers will be at each other's throats and in the process, they will strip Europe barer than a swarm of locusts. The depredations of the Thirty Years' War compressed into three to four years and extended over the entire continent; famine, disease, the universal lapse into barbarism, both of the armies and the people, in the wake of acute misery; irretrievable dislocation of our artificial system of trade, industry and credit, ending in universal bankruptcy; collapse of the old states and their conventional political wisdom to the point where crowns will roll into the gutters by the dozen, and no one will be around to pick them up; the absolute impossibility of foreseeing how it will all end and who will emerge as victor from the battle . . . That is the prospect for the moment when the systematic development of mutual one upmanship in armaments reaches its climax and finally brings forth its inevitable fruits."[119]

Engels reckoned that whichever side England backed would win, but America would emerge victorious from the war and assume economic hegemony. He looked for revolutions in France and Germany as a consequence. Indeed, the only hope of stopping a long destructive war was if the Russians were defeated and then the people overthrew the Czar and made a revolutionary peace. As JD Huntley concluded[120], Engels' forecasts were "astonishingly accurate".

Engels on a proletarian revolution in Russia

Engels' forecast about Russia was based on his analysis of weakness and distortions of emerging Russian capitalism. In 1877, Marx had written to Russian revolutionaries that: "Now the question is: can the Russian obshchina, a form of primeval common ownership of land, even if greatly undermined [by capitalist developments], pass directly to the higher form of communist common ownership? Or must it, conversely, first pass through the same process of dissolution as constitutes the historical development of the West?" His answer was: "If the Russian Revolution [overthrow of the Czar] becomes the signal for a proletarian revolution in the West, so that the two complement each other, the present Russian common ownership of land may serve as the starting point for communist development.[121]

In 1893, Engels referred to Marx's view and now added that any such possibility was no longer relevant, for the disappointing progress made by the Western proletarian movement was allowing time for the progress of Russian capitalism, thus rendering the obshchina option increasingly irrelevant. "No doubt the commune and to a certain extent the artel, contained germs which under certain conditions might have developed and saved Russia the necessity of passing through the torments of the capitalistic regime . . . I fully subscribe to our author's letter [Marx]. But in his, as well as in my opinion, the first condition required to bring this about was the impulse from without, the change of economic system in the Occident of Europe, the destruction of the capitalist system in the countries where it had originated. Our author [sic] said in a certain preface to a certain old manifesto, in January 1882, replying to the question whether the Russian commune might not be the starting-point of a higher social development: if the change of economic system in Russia coincides with a change of economic system in the West – so that the two complement each other, the present Russian common ownership of land may serve as the starting-point for communist development."

But, Engels said in 1893, "If we in the West had been quicker in our own economic development, if we had been able to upset the capitalistic regime some ten or twenty years ago, there might have been time yet for Russia to cut short the tendency of her own evolution towards capitalism. Unfortunately we are too slow, and those economic consequences of the capitalistic system which must bring it up to the critical point, are only just now developing in the various countries about us: while England is fast losing her industrial monopoly, France and Germany are approaching the industrial level of England, and America bids fair to drive them all out of the world's market both for industrial and agricultural produce."[122]

The following year, in an afterword to his On Social Relations in Russia [1875], Engels reserved judgment regarding the resilience of the commune system; nonetheless, even assuming the best case possible, a successful transition to communism in Russia based on the commune would still require a "sudden change of direction in Western Europe. Further, the interdependence of the Western and Russian patterns of development there emphasized is again apparent, insofar as the overthrow of the Czarist regime – a requirement for progress by the peasantry – would encourage proletarian revolution in the West, which in turn is represented as a necessary condition for a "socialist transformation" in Russia. Thus Engels posed the basis of the theory of permanent revolution as espoused by Russian revolutionary Leon Trotsky in the early 1900s.

Engels on the colonial revolution

While Engels was increasingly doubtful about the prospects of the Russian revolution starting before 'the West', he did expect the emergence of movements in the so-called colonial world as the result of what we now call 'globalisation'. "[O]wing to the continual cheapening of the price of industrial products as a result of machine labour, the old system of manufacture or industry founded upon manual labour was completely destroyed in all countries of the world. All semi-barbarian countries, which until now had been more or less outside historical development and whose industry had until now been based on manufacture, were thus forcibly torn out of their isolation. They bought the cheaper commodities of the English and let their own manufactory workers go to ruin. Thus countries that for thousands of years had made no progress, for example India, were revolutionized through and through, and even China is now marching towards a revolution. It has reached the point that a new machine invented today in England, throws millions of workers in China out of work within a year. Large-scale industry has thus brought all the peoples of the earth into relationship with one another, thrown all the small local markets into the world market, prepared the way everywhere for civilization and progress, and brought it about that everything that happens in the civilized countries must have its repercussions on all other countries."

As a result, "if now in England or France the workers liberate themselves, this must lead to revolutions in all other countries, which sooner or later will also bring about the liberation of the workers in those countries."

There was a great period of 'globalisation' (international trade and capital flows) from the end of the long depression of the 1880s. But after the first world war and the subsequent Great Depression of the 1930s capitalism turned inwards, with protectionism and nationalism. The post-1945 period under US hegemony saw a revival and expansion of world trade and also the explosion of colonial revolutions of Asia, Africa and Latin America, particularly China. From the 1980s, there was a new wave of trade and capital flows not seen since one hundred years earlier; but also producing a massive increase in the size of the global proletariat – to over 3.5 billion workers in industry and services. Indeed, the globalisation of capitalism has now reached the point where anything that happens in a major economy will have repercussions on all, as Engels forecast.[123]

Engels on military spending
Engels was regarded by his friends and Marx's family as an expert on military matters – "the General" he was nicknamed - having fought in the unsuccessful insurrectionary battles of the European revolutions of 1848. Now in the 1890s, he reckoned that militarism would bring about its own destruction by freeing states to compete and build armies with the latest technology that would be "devilishly expensive". Engels argued that 'force cannot make any money'; at most, it can take away money that has already been made. Money can only be provided through the medium of economic production. So nothing is more dependent on economic pre-requisites than precisely an army and navy".[124] Engels emphasised that 'milex' had no direct or indirectly positive effect on an economy; on the contrary it could increase financial frailties.[125]

Whether military spending is beneficial to a capitalist economy or is a burden on productive development has been an issue of debate among Marxists and others since. Was the 'military-industrial complex', so-called by US President Eisenhower in the 1950s, a key factor

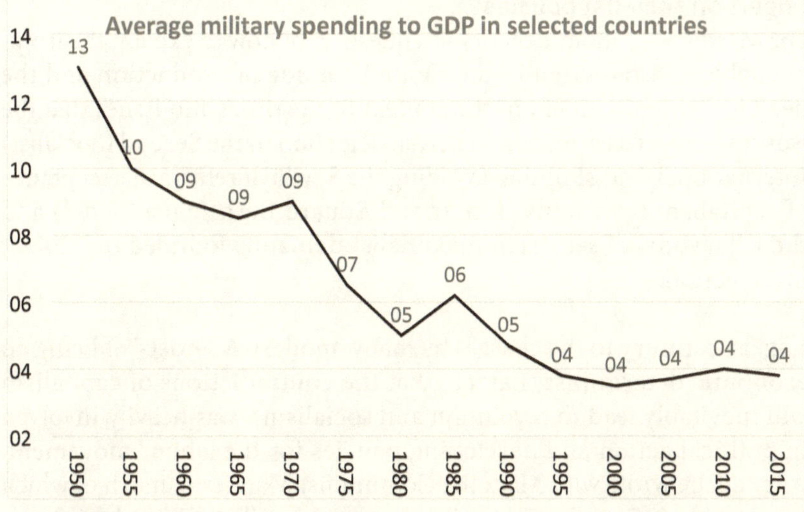

in the Golden Age for capitalism of the 1950s and 1960s, or was it, as Engels suggested, merely the beneficiary of an upswing in capitalism production.

Recent work by Adam Elveren appears to back a modified view of Engels' position of the role of military spending in a capitalist economy.[126] It may act to lower the rate of profit on capital and thus on economic growth as it did in the neo-liberal period of the 1980s onwards, when investment and economic growth slowed. But it can also help bolster the rate of profit through the state's redistribution of value from labour to capital, when labour is forced to pay more in taxation, or the state borrows more in order to boost investment and production in the military sector.

In the greater scheme of things, according to Elveren, milex is not decisive for the health of the capitalist economy, as Engels also argued. At its height, its share in GDP reached an average of 13%. But that was due to the Korean war. Even during the cold war period, that share fell by half to around 6% of GDP. With the collapse of the Soviet Union, military spending in the major imperialist powers halved again to 3%. Milex is not going to decide the future of capital, one way or the other. But thanks to Elveren's work, we have a much clearer picture of the economics of war and military spending beneath the horrors of its outcomes.

Engels on socialist policies

For Marxists, economic theory is a question of how to explain the irreconcilable contradiction in the capitalist mode of production and the need for its replacement in the context of the times and issues that the working-class faces. Engels, in his participation in the Second (Socialist) International, was skilful in avoiding the Scylla of reformist acceptance of capitalism (which his close friend Eduard Bernstein adopted) and the Charybdis of sectarian maximalist demands founded on violent insurrection.

Engels, contrary to the charges by many 'modern Marxists' of being an economic determinist (namely that the contradictions of capitalism will inevitably lead to revolution and socialism), was heavily involved in political action and developing policies for the labour movement. After all, he wrote with Marx the Communist Manifesto, much of which was based on Engel's own earlier document called, The Principles of Communism.[127]

In his post-Marx period, Engels reiterated his view first expressed as early as 1845 in the Condition that trade unions were necessary as the daily defenders of the working class in class struggle – hardly a 'determinist' position. But he did say that the labour movement should lose the meaningless slogan "A Fair Day's Wages for a Fair Day's Work" since capitalism's internal nature prevents capitalists from being "fair" to the workers whose wages they must continually seek to depress — and instead take up the slogan: "Possession of the means of work — raw material, factories, machinery — by the working people themselves!"

Engels took temporal precedence over Marx: "Engels was the first who endeavoured to give a theoretical exposition of the course of trade union development among the workers. Differing from the economists and socialists of his day, he showed as early as 1845 that trade unions are the inevitable result of the struggle between workers and industrialists, and that trade unions must form the basis of all working-class organisation"[128]

But Engels argued that, as they were a form of working-class organization arising from capitalist development itself, unions "naturally cannot alter the economic law according to which wages are determined by the relation between supply and demand in the labour market". Unions sought to reduce labour supply and competition among workers by the enforcement of uniform wages, but in fact "remain powerless against all great forces" that influence the supply–demand relation. This weakness is manifest in periods of crisis when competition between manufacturers to cut costs is at a pitch; only "under average conditions" are efforts to cut wages "somewhat restricted by the opposition of the working-men," whereas "in a time of considerable increase in the demand for labour, [a union] cannot fix the rate of wages higher than would be reached spontaneously by the competition of the capitalists among themselves."

But how to take the struggle for socialism beyond the limits of the trade unions? Engels outlined his answer in the debates with various socialist groups in the 1890s. "The English Social-Democratic Federation is, and acts, only like a small sect. It is an exclusive body. It has not understood how to take the lead of the working-class movement generally, and to direct it towards socialism. It has turned Marxism into an orthodoxy. Thus it insisted upon John Burns unfurling the red flag at the dock strike, where such an act would have ruined the whole movement, and, instead of gaining over the dockers, would have driven them back into the arms of the capitalists. We don't do this."

"Yet our programme is a purely socialist one. Our first plank is the social-isation of all the means and instruments of production. Still, we accept anything which any government may give us, but only as a payment on account, and for which we offer no thanks. We always vote against the Budget, and against any vote for money or men for the Army. In constituencies where we have not had a candidate to vote for on the second ballot, our supporters have been instructed to vote only for those candidates who pledged to vote against the Army Bill, any increased taxation, and any restriction on popular rights." Such tactics are worth bearing in mind in the vagaries of modern politics.

Engels after Marx's death made some significant steps forward in using Marxian political economy to analyse trends in late 19th century cap-italism. He discerned the long depression that the advanced capitalist economies entered in the 1870s and 1880s; he predicted the end of British economic hegemony as a result; he forecast the rise of imperialist rivalry and world war; and the resulting anti-colonial revolutions; he analysed the role of arms spending in capitalist economies and carefully developed socialist economic policy in a way that could unite organised workers in struggle – all this was no mean feat by Marx's surviving collaborator.

CHAPTER 7

The value from Engels

Friedrich Engels was the first to raise a theory of value and analyse the nature of capitalist competition, before Marx. "As long ago as 1844 I stated that the above-mentioned balancing of useful effects and expenditure of labour on making decisions concerning production was all that would be left, in a communist society, of the politico-economic concept of value."[129]

Engels chided a correspondent for dubbing the author of The Condition of the Working Class as "the father of descriptive economics": "You will find descriptive economics in Petty, Boisguillebert, Vauban, and Adam Smith, to name only a few. Such accounts, notably of proletarian conditions, were written by Frenchmen and Englishmen before I did mine. It was just that I was lucky enough to be precipitated into the heart of modern large-scale industry and to be the first whose eyes were opened to its implications – at any rate the most immediate ones."[130]

Engels offered more than just descriptive economics. It was he who put forward the concept of the 'reserve army of labour' which became central to Marx's explanation of wages and accumulation in capitalist booms and slumps. In his preface to Capital, Engels referred to "the displacement of millions of manual workers by a few machine-workers . . . [and] more and more of the machine-workers themselves," resulting in "the production of a number of available wage-workers in excess of the average needs of capital, the formation of a complete industrial reserve army, as I called it in 1845, available at the times when industry is working at high pressure, to be cast out upon the street when the inevitable crash comes, a constant dead weight upon the limbs of the working class in its struggle for existence with capital, a regulator for the keeping of wages down to the low level that suits the interests of capital"[131]

From his experience of working-class action in industrial Manchester, he championed the role of trade unions is fighting for better wages and conditions and for maintaining labour's share of income.

Engels took Marx's theory of rent and applied it to the burning issue of housing for working people, in particular exposing the fault-lines in the idea of owner-occupation through mortgages or fighting for 'fair rents' as opposed to public ownership of housing.

He defended Marx's law of profitability against all comers and its importance in crises of overproduction that capitalist accumulation generated.

In particular, Engels identified the regular and recurring cycles of boom and slump under capitalism and how they were related to the turnover of fixed capital.

He coined the term 'fictitious capital' to describe capitalist investment in financial assets like stocks and bonds and the role of fictitious capital in expanding accumulation, but also in sparking crises in production. Marx took up these ideas in Capital.

Additionally, he recognised the tendency towards the concentration and centralization of capital as well as the role of market speculation.

Lastly, Engels analysed the inefficient character of the capitalist economy and the superiority of a planned economy.

After Marx's death, Engels raised the growing risk of imperialist rivalry as Britain lost its hegemonic position in world capitalism and forecast a world war ahead.

He popularised and promoted Marxist theory and strategy in the international labour movement. As he coined it: "An ounce of action is worth a ton of theory."

Engels's claim to recognition is reinforced by an exceptional contribution in the 1840s (Umrisse) to the very foundations of the Marxian enterprise, a contribution entailing not only the "vision" but some of the building blocks in the working out of that vision. Subsequently, he proved himself to be a sophisticated interpreter of the doctrine of historical materialism and an important contributor in his own right.

As Marx said: "Without you, I would never had been able to bring the work to a conclusion, and I can assure you it always weighed like a nightmare on my conscience that you were allowing your fine energies to be squandered and to rust in commerce, chiefly for my sake, and, into the bargain, that you had to share all my petites miseres."[132]

One biographer has argued that Engels saw in himself a certain indolence "en fait de theorie," which proved to him that he was not qualified to work out an economic or philosophical system and to grapple it together with hooks of steel. "It is true that he had a natural talent for observing theoretical connexions, but he was content to grasp them by intuition, to understand the direction in which they pointed, and especially to draw inferences from them to action – for action was for him the crown of life. ... He could give himself up with passionate interest to scientific study. But the faculties of research and of logical analysis were less developed in him than the talent for stimulating, disseminating, and popularizing, in the noblest sense of the word." [133] But this seems to me a little harsh, as harsh as Engels was on his own contribution.

Engels attracts much hatred among some Marxists[134]. The reason seems to be that is that he turned Marxism into a theoretical system to transform a mass political movement. Many Marxist 'academics' do not like this. For this reason, they try to portray Marx as a "liberal thinker"[135]as opposed to the "sneaky" Communist Engels. It is true that Engels became a communist before Marx. But it is equally true that Marx and Engels are co-founders of Marxism and the Communist movement. This bond cannot be broken, despite the critics, in my view.

On learning from Kautsky that Rudolf Meyer proposed to describe him in an article as the "oldest and greatest of the living political economists," Engels protested: "To apply that epithet to me is really very silly. You would be doing a kindness to me and certainly to others as well, if you pointed out to him, at any rate for future guidance, that he must accustom himself to our less grandiose terminology."[136]

Returning Engels to Manchester

Engels lived in Manchester for more than two decades in the mid-19th century, honing his revolutionary philosophy through his observations of the horrific conditions endured by the working children, women and men in that cradle of industrial capitalism. But until recently there was no permanent marker to him in the city, no visual symbol of the man at all – despite the fact that his Manchester-forged thinking changed the course of 20th-century history.[137] Then in 2017, the Berlin-based, British-born artist Phil Collins transported a 3.5 metre statue of Friedrich Engels from a village in eastern Ukraine, through Europe, to Britain on a flat-bed truck and got permission to erect it in central Manchester. Collins: "Manchester is a meeting point. It represents both the birth of capitalism and the factory system and the magic of capitalism, the magic of surplus value. But Manchester is also a site of resistance to that – of the Chartists and the 1842 general strike and the suffragettes and the Vegetarian Society," he says. It's this latter, radical side of the city that can't be found, says Collins, among its memorials and statues and street names. The sculpture of Engels will subtly shift the balance."

Engels' stated personal motto: "take it easy";
favourite virtue: "jollity".

At this time of COVID-19 pandemic, it is apposite to return to one of Engels' great works: The Part played by Labour in the Transition from Ape to Man. In this piece, unfinished, Engels explains that man's labour is what makes humanity, but he also shows the intimate connection between human labour and nature – a connection that if disrupted would devastating to humanity as well as to the other species of the planet.

> "at every step we are reminded that we by no means rule over nature like a conqueror over a foreign people, like someone standing outside nature – but that we, with flesh, blood and brain, belong to nature, and exist in its midst, and that all our mastery of it consists in the fact that we have the advantage over all other creatures of being able to learn its laws and apply them correctly."

The Part played by Labour in the Transition from Ape to Man (1876)

This article was intended to introduce a larger work which Engels planned to call Die drei Grundformen der Knechtschaft – Outline of the General Plan. *Engels never finished it, nor even this intro, which breaks off at the end. It would eventually be included in* Dialectics of Nature.

Labour is the source of all wealth, the political economists assert. And it really is the source – next to nature, which supplies it with the material that it converts into wealth. But it is even infinitely more than this. It is the prime basic condition for all human existence, and this to such an extent that, in a sense, we have to say that labour created man himself.

Many hundreds of thousands of years ago, during an epoch, not yet definitely determinable, of that period of the earth's history known to geologists as the Tertiary period, most likely towards the end of it, a particularly highly-developed race of anthropoid apes lived somewhere in the tropical zone – probably on a great continent that has now sunk to the bottom of the Indian Ocean.[1]

First, owing to their way of living which meant that the hands had different functions than the feet when climbing, these apes began to lose the habit of using their hands to walk and adopted a more and more erect posture. This was the decisive step in the transition from ape to man.

All extant anthropoid apes can stand erect and move about on their feet alone, but only in case of urgent need and in a very clumsy way. Their natural gait is in a half-erect posture and includes the use of the hands. The majority rest the knuckles of the fist on the ground and, with legs drawn up, swing the body through their long arms, much as a cripple moves on crutches. In general, all the transition stages from walking on all fours to walking on two legs are still to be observed among the apes today. The latter gait, however, has never become more than a makeshift for any of them.

---

1 Darwin has given us an approximate description of these ancestors of ours. They were completely covered with hair, they had beards and pointed ears, and they lived in bands in the trees.

It stands to reason that if erect gait among our hairy ancestors became first the rule and then, in time, a necessity, other diverse functions must, in the meantime, have devolved upon the hands. Already among the apes there is some difference in the way the hands and the feet are employed. In climbing, as mentioned above, the hands and feet have different uses. The hands are used mainly for gathering and holding food in the same way as the fore paws of the lower mammals are used. Many apes use their hands to build themselves nests in the trees or even to construct roofs between the branches to protect themselves against the weather, as the chimpanzee, for example, does. With their hands they grasp sticks to defend themselves against enemies, or bombard their enemies with fruits and stones. In captivity they use their hands for a number of simple operations copied from human beings. It is in this that one sees the great gulf between the undeveloped hand of even the most man-like apes and the human hand that has been highly perfected by hundreds of thousands of years of labour. The number and general arrangement of the bones and muscles are the same in both hands, but the hand of the lowest savage can perform hundreds of operations that no simian hand can imitate – no simian hand has ever fashioned even the crudest stone knife.

The first operations for which our ancestors gradually learned to adapt their hands during the many thousands of years of transition from ape to man could have been only very simple ones. The lowest savages, even those in whom regression to a more animal-like condition with a simultaneous physical degeneration can be assumed, are nevertheless far superior to these transitional beings. Before the first flint could be fashioned into a knife by human hands, a period of time probably elapsed in comparison with which the historical period known to us appears insignificant. But the decisive step had been taken, *the hand had become free* and could henceforth attain ever greater dexterity; the greater flexibility thus acquired was inherited and increased from generation to generation.

Thus the hand is not only the organ of labour, *it is also the product of labour*. Only by labour, by adaptation to ever new operations, through the inheritance of muscles, ligaments, and, over longer periods of time, bones that had undergone special development and the ever-renewed employment of this inherited finesse in new, more and more complicated operations, have given the human hand the high degree of perfection required to conjure into being the pictures of a Raphael, the statues of a Thorwaldsen, the music of a Paganini.

But the hand did not exist alone, it was only one member of an integral, highly complex organism. And what benefited the hand, benefited also the whole body it served; and this in two ways.

In the first place, the body benefited from the law of correlation of growth, as Darwin called it. This law states that the specialised forms of separate parts of an organic being are always bound up with certain forms of other parts that apparently have no connection with them. Thus all animals that have red blood cells without cell nuclei, and in which the head is attached to the first vertebra by means of a double articulation (condyles), also without exception possess lacteal glands for suckling their young. Similarly, cloven hoofs in mammals are regularly associated with the possession of a multiple stomach for rumination. Changes in certain forms involve changes in the form of other parts of the body, although we cannot explain the connection. Perfectly white cats with blue eyes are always, or almost always, deaf. The gradually increasing perfection of the human hand, and the commensurate adaptation of the feet for erect gait, have undoubtedly, by virtue of such correlation, reacted on other parts of the organism. However, this action has not as yet been sufficiently investigated for us to be able to do more here than to state the fact in general terms.

Much more important is the direct, demonstrable influence of the development of the hand on the rest of the organism. It has already been noted that our simian ancestors were gregarious; it is obviously impossible to seek the derivation of man, the most social of all animals, from non-gregarious immediate ancestors. Mastery over nature began with the development of the hand, with labour, and widened man's horizon at every new advance. He was continually discovering new, hitherto unknown properties in natural objects. On the other hand, the development of labour necessarily helped to bring the members of society closer together by increasing cases of mutual support and joint activity, and by making clear the advantage of this joint activity to each individual. In short, men in the making arrived at the point where *they had something to say* to each other. Necessity created the organ; the undeveloped larynx of the ape was slowly but surely transformed by modulation to produce constantly more developed modulation, and the organs of the mouth gradually learned to pronounce one articulate sound after another.

Comparison with animals proves that this explanation of the origin of language from and in the process of labour is the only correct one. The little that even the most highly developed animals need to communicate to each other does not require articulate speech. In its natural state, no animal feels handicapped by its inability to speak or to understand human speech. It is quite different when it has been tamed by man. The dog and the horse, by association with man, have developed such a good ear for articulate speech that they easily learn to understand any language within their range of concept. Moreover, they have acquired the capacity for feelings such as affection for man, gratitude, etc., which were previously foreign to them. Anyone who has had much to do with such animals will hardly be able to escape the conviction that in many cases they now feel their inability to speak as a defect, although, unfortunately, it is one that can no longer be remedied because their vocal organs are too specialised in a definite direction. However, where vocal organs exist, within certain limits even this inability disappears. The buccal organs of birds are as different from those of man as they can be, yet birds are the only animals that can learn to speak; and it is the bird with the most hideous voice, the parrot, that speaks best of all. Let no one object that the parrot does not understand what it says. It is true that for the sheer pleasure of talking and associating with human beings, the parrot will chatter for hours at a stretch, continually repeating its whole vocabulary. But within the limits of its range of concepts it can also learn to understand what it is saying. Teach a parrot swear words in such a way that it gets an idea of their meaning (one of the great amusements of sailors returning from the tropics); tease it and you will soon discover that it knows how to use its swear words just as correctly as a Berlin costermonger. The same is true of begging for titbits.

First labour, after it and then with it speech – these were the two most essential stimuli under the influence of which the brain of the ape gradually changed into that of man, which, for all its similarity is far larger and more perfect. Hand in hand with the development of the brain went the development of its most immediate instruments – the senses. Just as the gradual development of speech is inevitably accompanied by a corresponding refinement of the organ of hearing, so the development of the brain as a whole is accompanied by a refinement of all the senses. The eagle sees much farther than man, but the human eye discerns considerably more in things than does the eye of the eagle. The dog has a far keener sense of smell than man, but it does not distinguish a hundredth part of the odours that for man are definite signs denoting different things. And the sense of touch, which the ape hardly possesses in its crudest initial form, has been developed only side by side with the development of the human hand itself, through the medium of labour.

The reaction on labour and speech of the development of the brain and its attendant senses, of the increasing clarity of consciousness, power of abstraction and of conclusion, gave both labour and speech an ever-renewed impulse to further development. This development did not reach its conclusion when man finally became distinct from the ape, but on the whole made further powerful progress, its degree and direction varying among different peoples and at different times, and here and there even being interrupted by local or temporary regression. This further development has been strongly urged forward, on the one hand, and guided along more definite directions, on the other, by a new element which came into play with the appearance of fully-fledged man, namely, *society*.

Hundreds of thousands of years – of no greater significance in the history of the earth than one second in the life of man [Engels note: A leading authority in this respect, Sir William Thomson, has calculated that little more than a hundred million years could have elapsed since the time when the earth had cooled sufficiently for plants and animals to be able to live on it.] – certainly elapsed before human society arose out of a troupe of tree-climbing monkeys. Yet it did finally appear. And what do we find once more as the characteristic difference between the troupe of monkeys and human society? Labour. The ape herd was satisfied to browse over the feeding area determined for it by geographical conditions or the resistance of neighbouring herds; it undertook migrations and struggles to win new feeding grounds, but it was incapable of extracting from them more than they offered in their natural state, except that it unconsciously fertilised the soil with its own excrement. As soon as all possible feeding grounds were occupied, there could be no further increase in the ape population; the number of animals could at best remain stationary. But all animals waste a great deal of food, and, in addition, destroy in the germ the next generation of the food supply. Unlike the hunter, the wolf does not spare the doe which would provide it with the young the next year; the goats in Greece, that eat away the young bushes before they grow to maturity, have eaten bare all the mountains of the country. This "predatory economy" of animals plays an important part in the gradual transformation of species by forcing them to adapt themselves to other than the usual food, thanks to which their blood acquires a different chemical composition and the whole physical constitution gradually alters, while species that have remained unadapted die out. There is no doubt that this predatory economy contributed powerfully to the transition of our ancestors from ape to man. In a race of apes that far surpassed all others in intelligence and adaptability, this predatory economy must have led to a continual increase in the number of plants used for food and the consumption of more and more edible parts of food plants. In short, food became more and more varied, as did also the substances entering the body with it, substances that were the chemical premises for the transition to man.

But all that was not yet labour in the proper sense of the word. Labour begins with the making of tools. And what are the most ancient tools that we find – the most ancient judging by the heirlooms of prehistoric man that have been discovered, and by the mode of life of the earliest historical peoples and of the rawest of contemporary savages? They are hunting and fishing implements, the former at the same time serving as weapons. But hunting and fishing presuppose the transition from an exclusively vegetable diet to the concomitant use of meat, and this is another important step in the process of transition from ape to man. A *meat diet* contained in an almost ready state the most essential ingredients required by the organism for its metabolism. By shortening the time required for digestion, it also shortened the other vegetative bodily processes that correspond to those of plant life, and thus gained further time, material and desire for the active manifestation of animal life proper. And the farther man in the making moved from the vegetable kingdom the higher he rose above the animal. Just as becoming accustomed to a vegetable diet side by side with meat converted wild cats and dogs into the servants of man, so also adaptation to a meat diet, side by side with a vegetable diet, greatly contributed towards giving bodily strength and independence to man in the making. The meat diet, however, had its greatest effect on the brain, which now received a far richer flow of the materials necessary for its nourishment and development, and which, therefore, could develop more rapidly and perfectly from generation to generation. With all due respect to the vegetarians man did not come into existence without a meat diet, and if the latter, among all peoples known to us, has led to cannibalism at some time or other (the forefathers of the Berliners, the Weletabians or Wilzians, used to eat their parents as late as the tenth century), that is of no consequence to us today.

The meat diet led to two new advances of decisive importance – the harnessing of fire and the domestication of animals. The first still further shortened the digestive process, as it provided the mouth with food already, as it were, half-digested; the second made meat more copious by opening up a new, more regular source of supply in addition to hunting, and moreover provided, in milk and its products, a new article of food at least as valuable as meat in its composition. Thus both these advances were, in themselves, new means for the emancipation of man. It would lead us too far afield to dwell here in detail on their indirect effects notwithstanding the great importance they have had for the development of man and society.

Just as man learned to consume everything edible, he also learned to live in any climate. He spread over the whole of the habitable world, being the only animal fully able to do so of its own accord. The other animals that have become accustomed to all climates – domestic animals and vermin – did not become so independently, but only in the wake of man. And the transition from the uniformly hot climate of the original home of man to colder regions, where the year was divided into summer and winter, created new requirements – shelter and clothing as protection against cold and damp, and hence new spheres of labour, new forms of activity, which further and further separated man from the animal.

By the combined functioning of hand, speech organs and brain, not only in each individual but also in society, men became capable of executing more and more complicated operations, and were able to set themselves, and achieve, higher and higher aims. The work of each generation itself became different, more perfect and more diversified.

Agriculture was added to hunting and cattle raising; then came spinning, weaving, metalworking, pottery and navigation. Along with trade and industry, art and science finally appeared. Tribes developed into nations and states. Law and politics arose, and with them that fantastic reflection of human things in the human mind – religion. In the face of all these images, which appeared in the first place to be products of the mind and seemed to dominate human societies, the more modest productions of the working hand retreated into the background, the more so since the mind that planned the labour was able, at a very early stage in the development of society (for example, already in the primitive family), to have the labour that had been planned carried out by other hands than its own. All merit for the swift advance of civilisation was ascribed to the mind, to the development and activity of the brain. Men became accustomed to explain their actions as arising out of thought instead of their needs (which in any case are reflected and perceived in the mind); and so in the course of time there emerged that idealistic world outlook which, especially since the fall of the world of antiquity, has dominated men's minds. It still rules them to such a degree that even the most materialistic natural scientists of the Darwinian school are still unable to form any clear idea of the origin of man, because under this ideological influence they do not recognise the part that has been played therein by labour.

Animals, as has already been pointed out, change the environment by their activities in the same way, even if not to the same extent, as man does, and these changes, as we have seen, in turn react upon and change those who made them. In nature nothing takes place in isolation. Everything affects and is affected by every other thing, and it is mostly because this manifold motion and interaction is forgotten that our natural scientists are prevented from gaining a clear insight into the simplest things. We have seen how goats have prevented the regeneration of forests in Greece; on the island of St. Helena, goats and pigs brought by the first arrivals have succeeded in exterminating its old vegetation almost completely, and so have prepared the ground for the spreading of plants brought by later sailors and colonists. But animals exert a lasting effect on their environment unintentionally and, as far as the animals themselves are concerned, accidentally. The further removed men are from animals, however, the more their effect on nature assumes the character of premeditated, planned action directed towards definite preconceived ends. The animal destroys the vegetation of a locality without realising what it is doing. Man destroys it in order to sow field crops on the soil thus released, or to plant trees or vines which he knows will yield many times the amount planted. He transfers useful plants and domestic animals from one country to another and thus changes the flora and fauna of whole continents. More than this. Through artificial breeding both plants and animals are so changed by the hand of man that they become unrecognisable. The wild plants from which our grain varieties originated are still being sought in vain. There is still some dispute about the wild animals from which our very different breeds of dogs or our equally numerous breeds of horses are descended.

It goes without saying that it would not occur to us to dispute the ability of animals to act in a planned, premeditated fashion. On the contrary, a planned mode of action exists in embryo wherever protoplasm, living albumen, exists and reacts, that is, carries out definite, even if extremely simple, movements as a result of definite external stimuli. Such reaction takes place even where there is yet no cell at all, far less a nerve cell. There is something of the planned action in the way insect-eating plants capture their prey, although they do it quite unconsciously. In animals the capacity for conscious, planned action is proportional to the development of the nervous system, and among mammals it attains a fairly high level. While fox-hunting in England one can daily observe how unerringly the fox makes use of its excellent knowledge of the locality in order to elude its pursuers, and how well it knows and turns to account all favourable features of the ground that cause the scent to be lost. Among our domestic animals, more highly developed thanks to association with man, one can constantly observe acts of cunning on exactly the same level as those of children. For, just as the development history of the human embryo in the mother's womb is only an abbreviated repetition of the history, extending over millions of years, of the bodily development of our animal ancestors, starting from the worm, so the mental development of the human child is only a still more abbreviated repetition of the intellectual development of these same ancestors, at least of the later ones. But all the planned action of all animals has never succeeded in impressing the stamp of their will upon the earth. That was left for man.

In short, the animal merely *uses* its environment, and brings about changes in it simply by its presence; man by his changes makes it serve his ends, *masters* it. This is the final, essential distinction between man and other animals, and once again it is labour that brings about this distinction.

Let us not, however, flatter ourselves overmuch on account of our human victories over nature. For each such victory nature takes its revenge on us. Each victory, it is true, in the first place brings about the results we expected, but in the second and third places it has quite different, unforeseen effects which only too often cancel the first. The people who, in Mesopotamia, Greece, Asia Minor and elsewhere, destroyed the forests to obtain cultivable land, never dreamed that by removing along with the forests the collecting centres and reservoirs of moisture they were laying the basis for the present forlorn state of those countries. When the Italians of the Alps used up the pine forests on the southern slopes, so carefully cherished on the northern slopes, they had no inkling that by doing so they were cutting at the roots of the dairy industry in their region; they had still less inkling that they were thereby depriving their mountain springs of water for the greater part of the year, and making it possible for them to pour still more furious torrents on the plains during the rainy seasons. Those who spread the potato in Europe were not aware that with these farinaceous tubers they were at the same time spreading scrofula. Thus at every step we are reminded that we by no means rule over nature like a conqueror over a foreign people, like someone standing outside nature – but that we, with flesh, blood and brain, belong to nature, and exist in its midst, and that all our mastery of it consists in the fact that we have the advantage over all other creatures of being able to learn its laws and apply them correctly.

And, in fact, with every day that passes we are acquiring a better understanding of these laws and getting to perceive both the more immediate and the more remote consequences of our interference with the traditional course of nature. In particular, after the mighty advances made by the natural sciences in the present century, we are more than ever in a position to realise, and hence to control, also the more remote natural consequences of at least our day-to-day production activities. But the more this progresses the more will men not only feel but also know their oneness with nature, and the more impossible will become the senseless and unnatural idea of a contrast between mind and matter, man and nature, soul and body, such as arose after the decline of classical antiquity in Europe and obtained its highest elaboration in Christianity.

It required the labour of thousands of years for us to learn a little of how to calculate the more remote natural effects of our actions in the field of production, but it has been still more difficult in regard to the more remote social effects of these actions. We mentioned the potato and the resulting spread of scrofula. But what is scrofula compared to the effects which the reduction of the workers to a potato diet had on the living conditions of the popular masses in whole countries, or compared to the famine the potato blight brought to Ireland in 1847, which consigned to the grave a million Irishmen, nourished solely or almost exclusively on potatoes, and forced the emigration overseas of two million more? When the Arabs learned to distil spirits, it never entered their heads that by so doing they were creating one of the chief weapons for the annihilation of the aborigines of the then still undiscovered American continent. And when afterwards Columbus discovered this America, he did not know that by doing so he was giving a new lease of life to slavery, which in Europe had long ago been done away with, and laying the basis for the Negro slave trade. The men who in the seventeenth and eighteenth centuries laboured to create the steam-engine had no idea that they were preparing the instrument which more than any other was to revolutionise social relations throughout the world. Especially in Europe, by concentrating wealth in the hands of a minority and dispossessing the huge majority, this instrument was destined at first to give social and political domination to the bourgeoisie, but later, to give rise to a class struggle between bourgeoisie and proletariat which can end only in the overthrow of the bourgeoisie and the abolition of all class antagonisms. But in this sphere too, by long and often cruel experience and by collecting and analysing historical material, we are gradually learning to get a clear view of the indirect, more remote social effects of our production activity, and so are afforded an opportunity to control and regulate these effects as well.

This regulation, however, requires something more than mere knowledge. It requires a complete revolution in our hitherto existing mode of production, and simultaneously a revolution in our whole contemporary social order.

All hitherto existing modes of production have aimed merely at achieving the most immediately and directly useful effect of labour. The further consequences, which appear only later and become effective through gradual repetition and accumulation, were totally neglected. The original common ownership of land corresponded, on the one hand, to a level of development of human beings in which their horizon was restricted in general to what lay immediately available, and presupposed, on the other hand, a certain superfluity of land that would allow some latitude for correcting the possible bad results of this primeval type of economy. When this surplus land was exhausted, common ownership also declined. All higher forms of production, however, led to the division of the population into different classes and thereby to the antagonism of ruling and oppressed classes. Thus the interests of the ruling class became the driving factor of production, since production was no longer restricted to providing the barest means of subsistence for the oppressed people. This has been put into effect most completely in the capitalist mode of production prevailing today in Western Europe. The individual capitalists, who dominate production and exchange, are able to concern themselves only with the most immediate useful effect of their actions. Indeed, even this useful effect – inasmuch as it is a question of the usefulness of the article that is produced or exchanged – retreats far into the background, and the sole incentive becomes the profit to be made on selling.

Classical political economy, the social science of the bourgeoisie, in the main examines only social effects of human actions in the fields of production and exchange that are actually intended. This fully corresponds to the social organisation of which it is the theoretical expression. As individual capitalists are engaged in production and exchange for the sake of the immediate profit, only the nearest, most immediate results must first be taken into account. As long as the individual manufacturer or merchant sells a manufactured or purchased commodity with the usual coveted profit, he is satisfied and does not concern himself with what afterwards becomes of the commodity and its purchasers. The same thing applies to the natural effects of the same actions. What cared the Spanish planters in Cuba, who burned down forests on the slopes of the mountains and obtained from the ashes sufficient fertiliser for one generation of very highly profitable coffee trees – what cared they that the heavy tropical rainfall afterwards washed away the unprotected upper stratum of the soil, leaving behind only bare rock! In relation to nature, as to society, the present mode of production is predominantly concerned only about the immediate, the most tangible result; and then surprise is expressed that the more remote effects of actions directed to this end turn out to be quite different, are mostly quite the opposite in character; that the harmony of supply and demand is transformed into the very reverse opposite, as shown by the course of each ten years' industrial cycle – even Germany has had a little preliminary experience of it in the "crash"; that private ownership based on one's own labour must of necessity develop into the expropriation of the workers, while all wealth becomes more and more concentrated in the hands of non-workers; that [... the manuscript breaks off here.]

Bibliography

Engels' major works
These can be found on the Marxist Internet Archive, https://www.marxists.org/archive/marx/index.htm

Also nearly every article or work by Engels is available to download here. http://www.hetwebsite.net/het/profiles/engels.htm

Secondary works
Cyril Smith: file:///C:/Users/ToshibaT/OneDrive%20-%20Independent%20Strategy/Documents/ENGELS/Articles%20by%20Cyril%20Smith.pdf

Chris Arthur: file:///C:/Users/ToshibaT/OneDrive%20-%20Independent%20Strategy/Documents/ENGELS/382934670-Engels-Today-A-Centenary-Appreciation.pdf

Howard and King: A History of Marxian Economics: Volume I: 1883-1929 https://press.princeton.edu/books/hardcover/9780691634241/a-history-of-marxian-economics-volume-i

Lindsey German, Friedrich Engels, life of a revolutionary, https://www.counterfire.org/articles/history/20911-frederick-engels-life-of-a-revolutionary

Samuel Hollander, Friedrich Engels and Marxian Political Economy, https://www.cambridge.org/core/books/friedrich-engels-and-marxian-political-economy/65304165BD09B1EEEACC56E87568C9F3

JD Huntley, The Life and Thought of Friedrich Engels, Yale University Press, 1991.

Jerrold Siegel, Marx's Fate: the shape of a life, Princeton University Press, 1978

My works on Marxian Political Economy
M Roberts, The Great Recession - a Marxist view https://www.lulu.com/shop/michael-roberts/the-great-recession/paperback/product-6079458.html

M Roberts, The Long Depression, Haymarket, 2016 https://www.haymarketbooks.org/books/693-the-long-depression

G Carchedi and M Roberts, eds World in Crisis, Haymarket 2018 https://www.haymarketbooks.org/books/1216-world-in-crisis#:~:text=Make%20a%20donation%20to%20sustain%20Haymarket%20Books!&text=The%20most%20comprehensive%20empirically%20based,otherwise%20unbroken%20path%20toward%20prosperity

M Roberts, Marx 200: a review of Marx's economics 200 years after his birth, Lulu 2018 https://www.lulu.com/shop/michael-roberts/marx-200-a-review-of-marxs-economics-200-years-after-his-birth/paperback/product-23580530.html

Chart sources

P39 Average length of cycles   Source: Bank of England

P42 Real GDP per capita in England (2016 prices)   Source: Bank of England

P52 Share of top 1% in UK national income (%) and union membership (m) Source: ONS

P57 UK real GDP per worker and real wage (1770=100) Source: see note 26

P58 UK real profit rate (%) Source: see note 25

P59 UK real wage growth 10yr mov ave % Source: Bank of England

P60 Falling cost of technology (% chg) drives down labour share in GDP (%)

Source: Bank of England

P63 US unemployment rate (U4) and underemployment rate (U6) Source: BLS

P99 Current cost average age of US private nonresidential assets (yrs) Source: BEA NIPA

P101 Annual turnover of circulating capital Source: see note 78

P117 Railways stocks index   Source: see note 103

P122 Industrial production growth in depression years relative to growth in 1850-70

Source: see note 114

P123 Share of world manufacturing output (%) Source: see note 124

P124 Share of gross foreign assets (%) Source: see note 124

P127 UK rate of profit 1855-1900 (%) Source: M Roberts, World in Crisis, Chapter 6

P133 Average military spending in selected countries (% of GDP) Source: see note 127

Endnotes

1   https://newleftreview.org/issues/I106/articles/gareth-stedman-jones-engels-and-the-genesis-of-marxism

2   (4 July 1864; MECW 41: 546).56

3   Engels Outline of critique of political economy Written: in October and November 1843; first published: in the Deutsch-Französische Jahrbücher, 1844; Translated: by Martin Milligan; Transcribed: for the Internet by director, February 1996.

4   Classical economics or classical political economy is a school of thought in economics that flourished, primarily in Britain, in the late 18th and early-to-mid 19th century. Its main thinkers are held to be Adam Smith, Jean-Baptiste Say, David Ricardo, Thomas Robert Malthus, and John Stuart Mill. https://en.wikipedia.org/wiki/Classical_economics#:~:text=Classical%20economics%20or%20classical%20political,Malthus%2C%20and%20John%20Stuart%20Mill.

5   https://en.wikipedia.org/wiki/Utility

6   In the Deutsch-Franzozische Jahrbucher," referring to the Outlines (9 August 1862).

7   2018 Marx's Analysis of Ground-Rent: Theory, Examples and Applications Deepankar Basu Department of Economics, University of Massachusetts, dbasu@econs.umass.edu

8   See https://monthlyreview.org/2004/10/01/monopoly-capitalism/ and https://thenextrecession.wordpress.com/2020/08/01/taking-on-the-fearsome-foursome-and-market-power/

9   Bank of England: The UK recession in context — what do three centuries of data tell us? By Sally Hills and Ryland Thomas of the Bank's Monetary Assessment and Strategy Division and Nicholas Dimsdale of The Queen's College, Oxford.

10   Jonathan Swift: https://en.wikipedia.org/wiki/A_Modest_Proposal

11   Marx and Engels, The Holy Family

12   Rubel remarked that "Marx acknowledges himself to be a disciple of his friend whom, fifteen years later, he would praise for his 'brilliant Outline' ('l'esquisse geniale') of 1844

13   M Kratke https://www.researchgate.net/publication/339586496_Friedrich_Engels_oder_Wie_ein_Cotton-Lord_den_Marxismus_erfand

14   The Holy Family op cit

15   The Condition of the working class in England op cit

16   https://www.marxists.org/history/etol/writers/german/1994/xx/engels.htm

17   https://en.wikipedia.org/wiki/Otto_Bauer

18   The study by the centre-left Institute for Public Policy Research (IPPR)

19   OECD https://www.oecd.org/g20/topics/employment-and-social-policy/The-Labour-Share-in-G20-Economies.pdf

20   David Card, Falling Union Membership and Rising Wage Inequality: What's the Connection? NBER Working Paper No. 6520, April 1998

21   https://www.brookings.edu/bpea-articles/declining-worker-power-and-american-economic-performance/

22   Paul Krugman, https://krugman.blogs.nytimes.com/2012/12/26/capital-biased-technological-progress-an-example-wonkish/

23   Adam Smith, The Wealth of Nations

24   Carl Frey, https://www.eudemonicproject.org/ideas/worker-replacing-and-labour-augmenting-technological-change, The Technology Trap: Capital, Labor and Power in the Age of Automation. Princeton University Press. 2019.

25   Robert Allen, Engels' pause: Technical change, capital accumulation, and inequality in the British industrial revolution, https://www.sciencedirect.com/science/article/abs/pii/S0014498309000199?via%3Dihub#!

26   Feinstein, Charles H. (1998). "Pessimism Perpetuated: Real Wages and the Standard of Living in Britain during and after the Industrial Revolution". *The Journal of Economic History*. 58 (3): 625–658. doi:10.1017/S0022050700021100. JSTOR 2566618.

27   The Condition of the Working Class in England, 1209–2004 Author(s): Gregory Clark Source: Journal of Political Economy, Vol. 113, No. 6 (December 2005), pp. 1307-1340

28   HM Boot, Real Incomes of the British Middle Class, 1760-1850: The Experience of Clerks at the East India Company. *The Economic History Review*

29   https://thenextrecession.files.wordpress.com/2016/12/speech946.pdf

30   https://voxeu.org/article/economic-impacts-immigration-uk

31   Adam Smith, https://en.wikipedia.org/wiki/Adam_Smith

32   David Ricardo, https://en.wikipedia.org/wiki/David_Ricardo

33   Jean Sismondi, https://en.wikipedia.org/wiki/Jean_Charles_L%C3%A9onard_de_Sismondi

34   https://www.marxists.org/archive/marx/works/1894-c3/supp.htm

35   Anti-Duhring

36   See the brilliant account of the 'great money trick' by Robert Tressell in his book Ragged Trousered Philanthropists, reproduced in Marx 200, (2018) pp163-66.

37   Engels told Danielson in 1888.

38   See Marx 200, p95

39   Rodbertus, https://en.wikipedia.org/wiki/Johann_Karl_Rodbertus

40   See Marx 200 op cit, pp85-88

41   Loria, https://en.wikipedia.org/wiki/Achille_Loria

42   Samuelson, https://en.wikipedia.org/wiki/Paul_Samuelson and see Marx 200, pp81-85

43   Sraffa, https://en.wikipedia.org/wiki/Piero_Sraffa

44   Fireman, https://ideas.repec.org/p/hal/journl/hal-02504152.html Kritik der Marx'schen Werttheorie. In Jahrbücher für Nationalökonomie und Statistik, Dritte Folge, Bd. III, Jena 1892, 793-808

45   Werner Sombart, https://en.wikipedia.org/wiki/Werner_Sombart

46   Karl Popper, https://en.wikipedia.org/wiki/Karl_Popper

47   The Housing Question

48   Pierre-Joseph Proudhon https://en.wikipedia.org/wiki/Pierre-Joseph_Proudhon

49   Sax, https://en.wikipedia.org/wiki/Emil_Sax

50   Stuart Hodkinson (2012, 427- 8

51   Mülberger in *Der Volkstaat* February 10 1872]

52   Harvey, *Paris: Capital of Modernity*. By David Harvey. New York: Routledge, 2003 Accumulation by dispossession; Lapavitsas Profit without producing – see Marx 200 pp85-88

53   Prometheus, https://en.wikipedia.org/wiki/Prometheus In Greek mythology, Prometheus is known for his intelligence and for being a champion of humankind,[3] and is also seen as the author of the human arts and sciences generally.

54   Paul Burkett, https://monthlyreview.org/2014/12/01/paul-burketts-marx-and-nature-fifteen-years-after/

55   https://monthlyreview.org/product/karl_marxs_ecosocialism/

56   https://www.marxists.org/archive/marx/works/1839/03/telegraph.htm

57   https://www.marxists.org/archive/marx/works/1883/don/index.htm

58   https://en.wikipedia.org/wiki/Genocide_of_indigenous_peoples

59   https://thenextrecession.wordpress.com/2020/01/31/corinavirus-nature-fights-back/

60   Engels, Friedrich. 1892. "The Mark." http://tinyurl.com/6e58e7

https://www.marxists.org/archive/marx/works/1892/12/mark.htm

61   Cox, Susan Jane Buck. 1985, "No Tragedy on the Commons." Environmental Ethics 7. http://tinyurl.com/5bys8h

62   Marx 1998: 611n

63   https://climateandcapitalism.com/2008/08/25/debunking-the-tragedy-of-the-commons/

64   (to Engels, 30 April 1868; MECW 43: 24)

65   See Marx 200 pp37-45

66   See Allen and Roberts The Long Depression

67   Conrad Schmidt, https://www.marxists.org/archive/plekhanov/1898/conrad-schmidt.htm

68   See Roberts Marx 200 op cit

69   https://de.wikipedia.org/wiki/Georg_Christian_Stiebeling

70   For more on Stiebeling, see Howard and King (1989: 28–9). And see http://library.fes.de/pdf-files/bibliothek/bestand/a79-04021.pdf

71   Esteban Maito in World in Crisis, chapter 4 and M Roberts in World in Crisis, Chapter 6.

72   [in 1835, *On the Economy of Machinery and Manufactures*, p. 285]

73   (2 March 1858; MECW 40: 278).

74   (5 March 1858; MECW 40: 282).

75 The Long Depression, Chapter 12

76 P Jones http://gesd.free.fr/jonesp12.pdf

77 Brian Green https://theplanningmotive.com/category/turnover-formula/

78 "While it does not affect the sense of the trend, it softens its slope, especially for the Japanese case, in which the rate of profit is almost double if we consider the rotation." E Maito https://mpra.ub.uni-muenchen.de/59283/3/MPRA_paper_59283.pdf

79 Eugen Duhring, https://en.wikipedia.org/wiki/Eugen_D%C3%BChring

80 https://en.wikipedia.org/wiki/Karl_Kautsky

81 https://en.wikipedia.org/wiki/Eduard_Bernstein

82 https://en.wikipedia.org/wiki/Rosa_Luxemburg

83 Capital Vol 3. Chap 15

84 Roberts, Profits and investment, https://thenextrecession.files.wordpress.com/2018/03/the-profit-investment-nexus.docx

85 See S Mavroudeas, http://www.antiper.org/2020/09/10/mavroudeas-engels-marxism/

86 M. Heinrich http://digamo.free.fr/heinrich13.pdf and see the reply by Carchedi and Roberts, https://monthlyreview.org/commentary/critique-heinrichs-crisis-theory-law-tendency-profit-rate-fall-marxs-studies-1870s/.

87 R Roth https://brill.com/previewpdf/book/edcoll/9789004367159/BP000002.xml

88 Vollgraf C-E., Jungnickel J (2002) Marx in Marx's words'? On Engels's edition of the main manuscript of book 3 of capital. International Journal of Political Economy 32(1): 35–78.

89 Marcello Musto, https://journals.sagepub.com/doi/abs/10.1177/0486613409331465

90 Seigel, Marx's Fate, https://www.psupress.org/books/titles/0-271-00935-7.html

91 Fred Moseley, https://thenextrecession.files.wordpress.com/2014/11/moseley-intro-on-marxs-writings.doc

92 See D Besomi, https://papers.ssrn.com/sol3/papers.cfm?abstract_id=1936380

93 Karl Marx, *Capital*, vol. 1 (1867), p. 633.

94 "I have been telling Moore about a problem with which I have been racking my brains for some time now. However, he thinks it is insoluble, at least pro tempore, because of the many factors involved, factors which for the most part have yet to be discovered. The problem is this: you know about those graphs in which the movements

of prices, discount rates, etc. etc., over the year, etc., are shown in rising and falling zig-zags. I have variously attempted to analyze crises by calculating these ups and downs as irregular curves and I believed (and still believe it would be possible if the material were sufficiently studied) that I might be able to determine mathematically the principal laws governing crises. As I said, Moore thinks it cannot be done at present and I have resolved to give it up for the time being." Karl Marx, "Letter to Engels," May 31, 1873. Marx Engels Werke, Vol 33, P821

95   Karl Marx, *Collected Works* (1990), p. 44:504.Lawrence and Wishart, London

96   Marx, *Collected Works*, p. 29:105. Lawrence and Wishart, London

97   Marx, *Collected Works*, p. 40:279–81. Lawrence and Wishart, London

98   Karl Marx, *Capital*, vol. 3 (1895), p. 477n.

99   Hills and Thomas, the UK recession in context – what do three centuries of data tell us?, Bank of England Quarterly Bulletin

100   G Carchedi, Chapter 2, World in Crisis, op cit

101   Lapavitsas: "It is one of a few innovative ideas to come out of radical political economy in recent years. For one thing, it seems capable of relating the unusual features of the crisis to the secular growth of finance. For another, it gives insight into the structural transformation of capitalist economies with its attendant social implications." Financialisation and capitalist accumulation: Structural Accounts of the Crisis of 2007-9, Discussion Paper no 16, february. http://www.researchonmoneyandfinance.org/media/papers/RMF-16-Lapavitsas.pdf

102   Financialization as a Theory of Crisis in a Historical Perspective: Nothing New under the Sun Juan Pablo Mateo Tomé July 2011 working paper series Number 262, UMass Amherst PERI.

103   Two Bubbles and a Crisis: Britain in the 1840s, Gareth Campbell Queen's University Belfast, Belfast, BT7 1NN (gareth.campbell@qub.ac.uk)

104   James Narron and Donald P. Morgan, Crisis Chronicles: Railway Mania, the Hungry Forties, and the Commercial Crisis of 1847 JUNE 05, 2015

105   In many respects, the current Long Depression, as I call it, since 2008 is similar. See Roberts, The Long Depression

106   Fourier, Charles. *Théorie des quatre mouvements et des destinées générales* .(Theory of the four movements and the general destinies), appeared anonymously in Lyon in 1808

107   Bernstein op cit, 1993 [1899]: 83–4

108   HL Beales https://www.jstor.org/stable/2589917?seq=1

109   Hatton & Boyer New Estimates of British Unemployment, 1870–1913, Journal of Economic History 2002

110   SB Saul, https://www.palgrave.com/gp/book/9780333049723

111   The Long Depression p38-39

112   J Schumpeter, Business Cycles 1950: 41n.

113   See Roberts, The Long Depression p228.

114   ("Protection and Free Trade" (1888; MECW 26: 524; see editorial note MECW 6: 696 n. 246).

115   "The Ten Hours' Question," MECW 10: 271–3; "The English Ten Hours' Bill," MECW 10: 295–6

116   https://en.wikipedia.org/wiki/August_Bebel

117   See Roberts, the Euro crisis is a crisis of capitalism, in World in Crisis, ed Carchedi and Roberts (2018).

118   See H Grossman. The law of accumulation, Chapter 3, Part 2

119   Engels, 'Introduction to Sigismund Borkheim's pamphlet In Memory of the German Blood-and-Thunder Patriots, 1806–1807' [1887], in mecw : Volume 26, p. 451

120   JD Huntley, The Life and Thought of Friedrich Engels 1991

121   MECW 24: 426; also reproduced 1890, MECW 27: 54

122   Letter to Nikolai Danielson, 24 February 1893; MECW 50: 110–11)

123   See Roberts, The crisis of global capitalism today, Praxis, Brazil 2018

124   In his pamphlet Can Europe disarm? 1893

125   http://www.mlwerke.de/me/me22/me22_369.htm#KAP_I

126   https://thenextrecession.wordpress.com/2019/11/18/milex-and-the-rate-of-profit/

127   Huntley 70-71 op cit.

128   Ryazanoff 1930 [1922]: 113; see also Henderson 1989: 62–3).

129   Anti-Duhring

130   29 August 1887; MECW 48: 97).

131   Preface to Capital Volume One

132   Marx to Engels, 7 May 1867; MECW 42: 371

133   Meyer 1969 [1934]: 329–30)15

134   See Mavroudeas op cit for a survey of the critics.

135   T Carver, 1984

136   17 May 1892; MECW 49: 416

137   https://www.theguardian.com/artanddesign/2017/jun/30/phil-collins-why-i-took-a-soviet-statue-of-engels-across-europe-to-manchester?CMP=Share_iOSApp_Other

Marx 200

– a review of Marx's economics 200 years after his birth

Michael Roberts

THE LONG DEPRESSION

HOW IT HAPPENED, WHY IT HAPPENED, AND WHAT HAPPENS NEXT

MICHAEL ROBERTS

WORLD IN CRISIS

A GLOBAL ANALYSIS OF MARX'S LAW OF PROFITABILITY

EDITED BY GUGLIELMO CARCHEDI AND MICHAEL ROBERTS